## SWIMMING WITH MY FATHER

Tim Jeal, an acclaimed novelist and biographer, is the author of *Livingstone*, which was a *New York Times Book Review* Notable Book of the Year, and *Baden Powell*, described in the *Literary Review* as 'one of the most important biographies of recent years.' A former winner of the John Llewellyn Rhys Prize, he is currently writing a life of Henry Morton Stanley.

Further praise for *Swimming with My Father*:

'Quite wonderful. I hope it becomes a classic: it deserves to be. There's so much life in it and so much art artlessly presented. The structure is masterly. The seriousness and the lightness are fully captured. I was very moved and also at times I laughed aloud . . . It really is very, very good.' Melvyn Bragg

'This is a marvellous book: funny, vivid, immensely touching and beautifully constructed . . . What makes the book even more moving is a suspicion that Jeal is a natural stoic and that it has taken a lot for him to prise open his heart like this. Ultimately, all I can say is this: it was worth it.' John Preston, *Evening Standard*

'Few people have written so well or with so much compassion about what it is like watching elderly parents confront the indignities and vulnerability of illness and old age . . . Jeal has made the ordinariness of it both funny and sad.'
Caroline Moorehead, *Times Literary Supplement*

'A gem – beautifully written and astonishingly moving.'
Virginia Ironside

'Jeal writes with beautiful sympathy and matter-of-fact even-handedness about both parents to achieve a hauntingly memorable portrait . . . This small, subtle memoir is better stocked with love, humour, sympathy and understanding than a shelf-full of celebrity-stuffed ego-fests.'
Hugh Massingberd, *Mail on Sunday*

'Terribly moving and terribly funny, often at the same time ... A hugely enjoyable read.' Lynn Barber

'[Jeal's] raw material is riveting . . . He has succeeded – in an age when the glisten of spit on a parent's tomb is so much more fashionable than a bunch of flowers – in producing a sincere, frank and moving tribute to two very different, very queer people.' Alexander Waugh, *Spectator*

'A delightful jewel of a book, full of remarkable and poignant insights about that shifting ground of love and embarrass-ment, anger and admiration across which we all travelled with our parents.' *Hampstead & Highgate Express*

'How rare it is, especially at the moment, to find a memoir so full of love, so non-judgemental – though not uncritical – lacking entirely in bitterness or resentment. I did love his father . . . *Swimming with My Father* is witty, full of affection and understanding. Hurrah.' Margaret Forster

'Moving, funny and full of love – a totally personal account which somehow manages to be universal. It has already been described as a small masterpiece. There is no doubt that it will become a classic.' Ruth Gorb, *Camden New Journal*

'Let me simply urge readers not to miss this superbly written book.' Christopher Gray, *Oxford Times*

'Jeal is a careful and conscientious biographer, who turns on his own life the measured gaze he turned on Baden Powell. The book is great on the ungraspable mysteries of parents seen from the child's eye . . . The litany of detail paints a beautiful watercolour of a family – and a world – we will never see again.' Tim Guest, *Daily Telegraph*

'[A] concise essay on the nature of Englishness . . . This affecting memoir of growing up in the 1950s is partly a study in boyhood embarrassment, partly a touching elegy for a lost world of certainty and conscience.' *Observer*

'Throughout, Jeal's prose is lucid and spare. He chronicles his gradual understanding of his parents with love and respect . . . The unfailing consideration he displays towards his parents ensures that the honesty with which he describes their decline is redemptive rather than cruel.' Lillian Pizzichini, *New Statesman*

'This intensely personal offering is by turns wryly funny and achingly sad, hugely loving but never sentimental. A little book with a big heart, this is exquisite.' *Good Book Guide*

# Swimming with My Father
## *A Memoir*

### TIM JEAL

*faber and faber*

First published in 2004
by Faber and Faber Limited
3 Queen Square London WC1N 3AU

This paperback edition first published in 2005

Typeset by Faber and Faber Limited
Printed in England by Mackays of Chatham plc, Chatham, Kent

A CIP record for this book
is available from the British Library

ISBN 0-571-22101-7

# LIST OF ILLUSTRATIONS

vii

# Swimming with My Father

# ONE

My father loved to swim in rivers, and, in 1949, when I turned four and he forty-three, he started taking me with him. Recently I came across a small black and white photograph, taken of us both in that year, wading into the River Itchen near Winchester. We are wearing discreet torso-covering costumes – a style even then old-fashioned. I am pressing ahead, but only because the water is shallow. When it grew deeper, I would clutch his hand, and pray not to stub my toe on a stone or disappear into an underwater chasm. My father said that if I could only give myself up to the water, and believe it would support me, I would soon learn to swim. But it would be several years before I managed this act of faith, and until then I would depend on his help to stay afloat.

In the River Mole – his preferred watering place, since it was near Dorking, his childhood home – the water could be muddy and the bottom unpredictable. Often I lost my footing and swallowed loamy mouthfuls, the taste lingering in my mouth long after I had blown strands of snot from my nose and had dried myself. I was never truly afraid, even when out of my depth. My father's firm but gentle hands gave me a sense of complete security. I remember the prickly

3

feel of his bathing costume as he carried me shivering to the bank, and the shining drops nestling among the hairs on his chest. After wrapping me in a towel, he would return to the water and swim with leisurely strokes, plainly in his element.

Although I didn't enjoy river swimming, it never occurred to me to refuse to go with him. I can only suppose I didn't like to disappoint him, given the obvious pleasure it gave him to take me. My father was never less than kind and considerate to me, so I could hardly treat him differently.

I didn't know until a few years later that he belonged to a fellowship of Christian mystics – the Order of the Cross, whose few hundred members sought 'oneness with the all-pervading divine presence, the Father-Mother' – and that he felt closer to achieving this pantheistic objective in natural surroundings. Every day my father spent time alone in his room, meditating and then writing down his thoughts. A week after our swim, his meditation began: 'Be not merely in the river, but become part of it, through its penetration of one's whole Being . . . The purpose of my life is to partake of the same beauty as the stars and trees and flowers.'

On many weekends in summer, when I was between five and eight, my father and I caught a Southern electric train from west London to Dorking, and went walking for miles, hand in hand, in the Surrey countryside. Among my father's favourite childhood haunts were Box Hill, Leith Hill, The Nower, and Ranmore Common.

My father thought of the natural world as being like an inspiring, albeit flawed reflection of 'the real and perfect other world', which it palely mirrored. But the hills and valleys of this earth plainly delighted him. He would walk happily for hours, carrying me whenever I flagged, as satisfied to be squelching along muddy paths as climbing the springy turf of sunlit hillsides.

Because he believed in the essential 'oneness' of all life, my father was a vegetarian. Besides hating every kind of killing, he deplored all needless damage to inanimate nature. Trees he revered almost as if they were sentient beings, and he would often stand in silent awe listening to their sighs and whisperings. Sometimes he placed his arms around an ancient trunk as if embracing an old and trusted friend. This did not embarrass me. Nor was I bothered when he chose to sink down without warning in a patch of long grass, despite having been talking, moments earlier, to some passer-by. He liked to quote a verse from 'Reconciliation', written by the Irish mystical poet A. E. (William George Russell), which started: 'I begin through the grass once again to be bound to the Lord . . .'

While I never quite shared his absorption in his surroundings, I am still tantalized by memories of pigeons cooing in the vaulted dimness of thick hazel woods, and by my feeling at that time, that I, like the tangled shoots rising from the forest floor, was part of a living entity, far older and mightier than the family of man.

It was not until I was seven that I became embarrassed by my father's lack of self-consciousness. He had just discovered the Bates 'better sight without glasses' book and method. One exercise involved rolling the eyeballs in order to strengthen the internal muscles of the eye. Another, called 'palming', required one to place one's palms over both eyes and to imagine a starless night or black velvet. When my father chose to do these exercises, sitting beside me on a District Line train en route to Dorking via Wimbledon, I sat in silence, cheeks burning, convinced that our fellow passengers would think him crazy.

When I travelled with my mother on the tube or bus, things

5

would be very different. Sometimes, she would nudge me surreptitiously, indicating some comically dressed person, and then greatly enjoy my difficulties as I fought to keep a straight face. She herself could remain composed after saying the most outrageous things. If I'd ever laughed out loud, she would have told me I was being extremely rude, and would have meant it. While I might enjoy the sight of a fat man in a tight suit, and be entertained to see some elderly woman grotesquely made-up, I soon felt mean for being amused and thought of what my father would have said to me if he knew. He always found he had things in common with people, and never smiled at their expense. I liked this. But I also admired my mother's ability to look so innocent while making her funny and mischievous remarks.

One day, while standing with my father in Wimbledon Station near the glass case containing the stuffed dog that stood on the platform right through the 1950s, I told him how much it worried me when he did the Bates exercises in public. He looked flabbergasted.

'People might laugh at you,' I explained.

'I wouldn't mind if they did.'

'But I mind, daddy.'

'Do you really see people staring at me? What sort of person would do that?'

I thought of my mother. My father looked quite unhappy now. I wanted to tell him it was because I loved him that I cared what people thought. But just then the train came in, and soon we were with other people. I knew he had the Bates book with him and now felt he couldn't read it because I would get upset. I started to feel guilty. Maybe if people *had* noticed him rolling his eyes, it wouldn't have mattered. When we were approaching Dorking, I reached out a hand and was relieved he took it.

Whenever I passed a butcher's shop, I would think how sad the fate of the dead rabbits and other animals would make my father if he were passing instead of me. Having a father who did not eat meat, and loving, as a boy, the anthropomorphic goings-on in the *Little Grey Rabbit* books, I would view butchers' displays with dismay. But even then, I ate meat at home, sometimes.

My mother told me that animals ate each other and that humans were animals – albeit very superior ones – and that meat was good for us and had been eaten by us since we all lived in caves, so it was silly not to follow our ancestors' example. When I told my father what my mother had said, he replied that our advanced minds and sense of right and wrong gave us choices no animal had. People in England had once killed thieves for stealing a few coins and so the past was no guide as to how to behave. Over the centuries, human beings, in most places, had become less cruel and in the end they would stop eating meat. Since both my parents felt strongly on the subject, a compromise came into being. I ate meat, but generally only when I was alone with my mother; and, in the evening, I usually ate a portion of the vegetarian food my mother had cooked for my father. This was no hardship since I loved the nut cutlets and the cheese and egg dishes he ate.

After I turned eight, I began to eat more meat, and there were evenings when only my father ate a vegetarian meal. I knew that if I had not eaten meat with my mother, she would have looked on me with disapproval. My father never commented on this change, and I loved him all the more for it.

In the mid-1970s, I moved from a house in Kentish Town to one in Hampstead. My father, now aged seventy, enjoyed cycling across London from Earl's Court to walk on the

Heath with me. In the summer he liked to swim in the men's pond, and sometimes I would accompany him, though, aged thirty, I was no keener on swimming than before. On a hot July day in 1977, we walked along the Lime Avenue together, towards the Highgate ponds. It was Sunday, and women in light summer dresses, children with their parents, and dogs and their owners were thronging the avenue. On our way, my father told me about his recent dealings with Kensington & Chelsea's planning department, interrupting himself occasionally to remark upon the beauty of this tree or that.

The boundary wall of my parents' back garden was also the rear wall of a row of mews cottages – about four of them – whose owners were often tempted to create new windows. My father would never force them to fill in these illicit openings in the party wall, but would agree a licence in each case, specifying a basic size and that the bottom sash should be fixed, so no-one could look down directly into his and my mother's garden. Every other year or so, some new, and generally larger, window would appear unheralded, and he would be obliged to seek out lawyers and planners to make some new agreement.

As we walked in the dappled shade under the limes, I gained the impression that my father was moving more slowly than usual. The surface of the avenue was quite rough, with flints and other irregular stones sticking up from the underlying clay. As if his legs had become heavy, my father seemed to find it an effort to lift his feet clear of these stones. I was about to remark on this when he began an anecdote that soon made me forget my worries.

On his previous visit to my house, he had discussed these wretched window licences with me, and had then made a list of points to raise with his planning officer. Rather than use a new sheet of paper, he had written these items on the back of a discarded page of the historical novel I had been working on at the time. On his next visit to the Town Hall, my father had handed this same list to the planner, who had read it and then glanced at the writing on the back. A look of amazement had spread across the man's features as he went on reading. When, at last, he returned the page to my father, he said with an arch grin: 'I imagine you'd like to have this back.' In the bus, on his way home, my father had glanced at my typed words for the first time and had been horrified to discover that the planning officer had just read the draft of a sexually explicit scene from my novel – presumably attributing authorship to him.

'I have to admit, he's been more attentive since then,' my father told me with the faintest of smiles.

At the men's pond, the sunbathing and changing areas were crowded, and the place stank of suntan oil, sweat and cigarette smoke. A number of men were oiling each other's backs, stomachs and, in one case, genitals. Even from where we were standing, I could clearly see a glistening erection. Fearing that a similar glimpse would ruin my father's afternoon, I clutched his arm, and muttering that it would be less crowded closer to the pond, ushered him firmly in that direction. I felt furious that I had to force him to a location where the ground was covered by duckboards which would hurt his feet. Yet when my father had undressed and was hobbling towards the pond across these excruciating slats, I forgot my indignation with the exhibitionists. Suddenly, it struck me that his old trouble with dropped metatarsals could not alone account for his snail-like progress to the water's edge.

Instead of diving in as usual, he used the steps, gingerly inching his way into the green water. Just when I was almost certain that something must be seriously wrong, he kicked-off strongly, and swam with powerful strokes towards the raft, leaving me gasping in his wake, as so often in the past.

But back on dry land, the length of time it took him to dress, and his shuffling gait, had me worrying again. He had towelled his hair vigorously and had forgotten to comb it, so his white locks stuck up crazily.

'How are you feeling?' I asked, as he stopped to rest.

'Maybe I've overdone it a bit.'

I willed myself to believe that his long and largely uphill cycle journey earlier in the day might indeed explain his leaden footsteps now, but my worries persisted.

He telephoned me a few days later to say that because I'd been 'so bothered' about him, he'd had himself assessed at the Nature Cure Clinic. The verdict, he told me, as if with papal infallibility, was that he was suffering from nothing more alarming than exhaustion and would be 'as fit as a flea in no time'.

'Fleas drink blood,' I reminded him.

He laughed. 'As a matter of fact I do have a new diet and some daily exercises.'

Since he was already getting plenty of exercise, and any diet prescribed at the clinic would be sure to consist of his usual nuts and vegetables, I couldn't see that there would be much change in his daily regimen. For years my father had been a member of the clinic's management committee, so I knew how little faith the staff had in conventional medical tests and treatments. He himself was implacably opposed to vivisection, and was reluctant to take any drugs in case they had been tried out on animals.

'Let's hope the diet does the trick,' I murmured, trying not to sound sceptical.

I expected further justification from my father to support the clinic's diagnosis. Sure enough he told me that his feet were entirely responsible for his difficulties in walking. But I wasn't to worry, because 'Tuggy' – Miss Tugwell, his gruff old chiropodist – was making him a foam and leather pad which would cushion the worst of his dropped metatarsals. He hoped to collect it when he next passed her pretty Regency house in Pelham Street, en route to Harrods, where he regularly bought fish for the stray cats which my mother had recently started enticing into the house. To meet the expensive challenge of feeding these animals (eleven in number, and rising), he had been cultivating an assistant in the food hall who now sold him fish at a huge discount, shortly before it would otherwise have been thrown away. I tried not to think of him cycling along the busy, fume-filled Cromwell Road, several times a week, with heavy packets of fish swinging precariously from his handlebars – especially if something really was wrong with his legs. Whatever the true state of his health, I couldn't help being depressed by the thought of his immense energy dwindling away.

Except for some brief and extremely Delphic religious utterances, usually separated by several years, my father had never tried to explain his religious beliefs to me. This reticence may have been due to the knowledge that his convictions had damaged his relationship with my down-to-earth mother. He must also have known that she would have fiercely resisted any efforts to convert me. I could easily have questioned my father about such matters, but had not done so to date. This was partly because it would have felt like a betrayal of my mother, and partly because I didn't feel the need. My father gave expression to his faith simply by living as he did, and by being himself.

My parents lived in the same mansion flat, and later in the same house, but always slept in separate rooms after my birth. Decades later, my mother told me they had never made love again after she became pregnant with me. Nor did they go out alone together to restaurants, theatres or cinemas. I cannot remember my parents, my sister and myself ever going out anywhere as a family. But my mother and father did entertain friends to dinner, accepted return invitations, and every summer shared a two-week holiday at our cottage in Cornwall – usually inviting guests to stay; otherwise my mother would spend hours in the garden, while my father slipped through the hedge to lie alone in the field.

By the time I was six or seven, I had seen other parents holding hands and even kissing decorously, which had started me wondering why my parents were so distant from one another. I could only suppose that something had happened between them years ago. One summer's day at this time, my mother announced at breakfast that she and I and my father would be going to the country in a hired car to 'tidy up' her parents' grave. Although I didn't know it, I was about to learn something significant about their past. But as we drove away, I was simply pleased that we were doing something together for once, and delighted that my mother and father were sitting side by side in the front of a car like other parents did. I had no idea that my father had only been asked to come with us because he was needed as our chauffeur, since my mother had never learned to drive.

The grave was in the churchyard of a nondescript village near Woking, with a confusingly metropolitan name, West End. My father disliked cars, and through much of my childhood did not own one. So, for this reason, and perhaps to economize, on this occasion he hired the smallest Austin he could find. My mother, wearing Wellingtons, a headscarf, and an old gardening overcoat embellished with a favourite brooch – her grandmother's intertwined initials in rubies and emeralds – ruminated aloud on whether she could manage to spot a second magpie, having just seen an unlucky first, and on whether she had remembered to turn off the gas. Meanwhile, I sat in the back, imagining Selina, our newly acquired Siamese cat, being splattered across the kitchen walls.

West End church resembled a chapel of rest in a cemetery more than a parish church, and the graveyard was equally forlorn. While my parents worked on opposite sides of the grave with shears, trowels and scrubbing brushes, my mother told me in a solemn voice that my grandfather had 'almost won' the Distinguished Service Order during the Boer War. I could see that it still upset her that he had not got this special medal years ago, so it surprised me that my father started to rake the granite chippings noisily, while she was still speaking.

'What's the matter with you?' my mother demanded.

'Not much,' muttered my father. 'I just wish you'd stop giving Tim the impression that killing foreigners and winning medals are the only worthwhile things in life.'

My mother smiled at him oddly, and yanked up a clump of grass from the gravel. Then she said to me in a voice that shook a little: 'Your father didn't want to fight in the war.'

'That's not fair, Norah. What I "wanted" didn't come into it.' My father had spoken calmly, in his usual manner, but I knew he wasn't feeling calm.

'Split hairs, if you like,' replied my mother, 'the plain fact is: to start with you refused to join up.'

My father murmured reassuringly in my direction: 'I'll tell you the whole story when we get home.'

I know if I'd reminded my father of his promise when we were back in London, he would have answered any question I might have put to him; but, for some reason, I decided not to put any. I suppose I was scared of learning something that might make me think less of him.

My parents brooded for a while at the graveside, neither speaking until my mother turned away from my father and resumed the story of my grandfather's disappointment. Apparently, if there had been another more important kind of soldier present to see him rescue a wounded man under fire, then the DSO medal would have been his. Instead, a less senior kind of soldier, a sergeant, had been the only one to witness my grandfather's brave act; and, strangely, this man had not counted. My mother seemed unsurprised by this odd rule that made some people's eyes more important than others. My grandfather – I would learn years later – had shared her attitude. Although he had risked his life to save a man from the ranks, in his view an unbridgeable gulf existed between officers and men. Indeed, he had illustrated it by taking his enormous dinner service and all his silver to South Africa, along with his wife and servants.

Today, as if parodying Transvaal picnics of long ago, my mother had filled a deep wicker hamper and squeezed it into the boot of our hired car. We now consumed its contents in the grounds of the nearby Gordon Boys' Home – founded as a national memorial to the martyr, General Gordon – and in recent years renamed the Gordon Boys' School.

I was alarmed by the grown-up-looking boys wandering about, and my unease must have showed, since my mother felt obliged to tell me that this was no ordinary school. It was a 'Home' for the sons of dead soldiers, and thirty years ago my grandfather had presided over it under the title of 'The Commandant' – a most 'unhomely' name, I'd thought. My grandmother died during her husband's reign at the Home, and this was how she came to be buried here, beneath a white marble cross, standing on a three step plinth. The inscription reads: Sacred to the memory of Constance Wilmot Annie, Dearly loved wife of Sir Thomas Pasley, Baronet and daughter of the 13th Earl of Huntingdon – making it sound, I thought, as though her father had been someone's daughter: 'baronet and daughter of . . .'. On the other side is an inscription devoted to my grandfather, who died a quarter of a century after his wife, and was buried in the same grave. A professional soldier, he had been adjutant and then brevet lieutenant-colonel of the Royal Berkshire Regiment, and had retired, at his own request, soon after the Boer War at the age of thirty-nine, returning briefly to the regiment during the Great War to take charge of newly enlisted men passing through the depot on their way to France.

My mother did not mention that at the time of my grandmother's death, she was living in 'The Commandant's House', trying, despite her father's opposition, to develop a singing career. Not until I was about twenty did I happen to find her book of newspaper cuttings and discovered that, after making her début at Leighton House in 1921, she had given recitals at the Wigmore Hall in 1923 and 1924, and had taken the part of Despina in a London production of *Cosi Fan Tutti* in 1925. *The Times's* music critic wrote of her having 'a very pretty soprano voice, small in range but sympathetic', and the *Daily Telegraph's* reviewer praised 'the purity and beauty of her tone and the ease with which it seemed to float'. Since her parents had never taken her to a single concert or opera, except Gilbert and Sullivan, it was a considerable achievement to have made a successful début at the age of nineteen. She had started singing lessons only a year earlier. Until then, her experience of classical music had been limited to *morceaux de salon*, which she had heard performed by aristocratic amateurs at her aunt, Lady Huntingdon's, charity concerts.

My grandfather thought professional musicians wholly unsuitable companions for his daughters. In addition, he had a conventional dread of the fabled sexual excesses of Italian tenors. So, while he had agreed to pay for my mother's singing lessons, he did not encourage her to continue her career after she had been launched. In his view, if ladies wanted to work, they should stick to the unpaid voluntary variety – an opinion he shared with most men of his class. For him, it was a highly convenient point-of-view to maintain. His wife's death had left him without a hostess to help entertain the many distinguished people who came to the Gordon Boys' Home. The Princess Royal was a frequent visitor, and was always shepherded round by my grandfather,

as were the Duke and Duchess of York, later King George VI and Queen Elizabeth. Sir Thomas made it clear to my mother that she ought to put him, and the nation's tribute to General Gordon, a long way before her singing career. The Gordon Boys' fathers had died serving the British Empire, and their sons deserved to live in an institution characterized not only by manly simplicity, but also by those refined and civilizing touches which only a lady could bestow.

Because my mother never spoke of her career, nor sang a note if she thought anyone was within earshot, I sensed that the subject was a painful one and never asked her why she gave up singing. I can only guess that her father's lack of support was one reason, and that another may have been her reluctance – after a sheltered education with a governess – to expose herself to the hardships and competitive pressures facing a professional opera singer and recitalist. Although the famous agency of Ibbs & Tillett had offered to promote her concerts, she soon decided to confine her singing to charity concerts. In future, snippets about her in newspapers would typically be headed: 'Earl's Niece Sings for Waifs and Strays Society.'

In 1930, my grandfather retired to a pleasant Georgian house in the Meon Valley in Hampshire, taking my mother with him. She was twenty-eight. Many of the eligible young men she might have married had been killed in the Great War, and her father's snobbery would narrow the field further. As a girl, my mother had been told by him that only a handful of children in the whole of Berkshire were 'suitable' to be invited over to play. In Hampshire, two decades later, Sir Thomas tried to be no less discriminating in respect of adult males.

My parents rarely spoke of how they first met. But although the facts caused my mother some embarrassment, when I was twelve she told me the story. In 1932, on a visit to London, to buy fabrics and furniture for their new home, my mother walked into Heal's furniture shop in the Tottenham Court Road and was mesmerized by a young man working there.

Although my father designed furniture for the shop – including something described in his school magazine as 'a remarkable chair-settee combination' – on the day he met my mother he was serving customers in the store, an activity my grandfather would have considered little better than sweeping the streets. Unaffected by such outmoded attitudes, my mother invited him to come to her Meon Valley home on the following weekend to advise her about modern furniture. Flattered, my father agreed to come. Seeing his gentle, intelligent face again, and hearing his pleasing voice, my mother knew she wanted to repeat the experience as soon as possible. Further meetings were arranged which had little to do with furniture.

An acrimonious struggle ensued between my mother and my grandfather. Although alarmed by it, my father's fears were conquered by love. My mother had given up her career for her father's sake, but she would not give up the man she now adored. So, in 1933, Sir Thomas was obliged to accept as his son-in-law a man without fortune or profession, and with a father 'in trade' – my paternal grandfather being the inattentive owner of an ailing haulage business. Worse still, although my father was well-spoken, he had not been educated at any of the schools my grandfather had heard of. Dorking High School sent pupils to Oxford and Cambridge every year, but this was of no interest to him. The fact that my father's father was chairman of the school's governors, a Justice of the Peace, Leader of the Council, a County Councillor, and owned a large house and a street in the town, did not impress my grandfather, who thought small towns, and everything to do with them, insufferably *infra dig*.

In 1934, Sir Thomas Pasley took a flat in Church Street, Kensington, large enough to accommodate, along with himself and my parents, any child they might have, this child's nanny, a couple of guests, a cook and a maid. Ostensibly so that my father would be able to earn more money – and also so that he would not embarrass his new family by being seen working in a shop – a change of job was arranged. A successful old boy of Dorking High School, James Chuter

Ede MP – a good friend of my father's father and soon to be a government minister – also happened to be chairman of the London and Home Counties Joint Electricity Council. With his help, my father slipped into a job in the Electricity Council's London headquarters in the Aldwych. I do not know what dull clerical tasks my father performed in the Council's legal department, but, at any rate, they constituted respectable office work, which he quickly came to detest.

Monday to Friday, no matter the season, my father ran to work through Kensington Gardens, swimming in the Serpentine en route, before running on through Hyde Park, Green Park, and then St James's Park, carrying his City clothes in a case. If he attracted any attention, this would have been because jogging was unknown at the time. He made no spectacle of himself by hugging trees or lying in the grass. But, if my maternal grandfather had happened to read, in an old notebook belonging to my father, among personal jottings and sketches of furniture, a striking passage from Sir Thomas Browne's *Religio Medici*, he might have felt a shiver of foreboding.

'There is surely,' began my father's chosen quotation, 'a piece of divinity in us – something that was before the elements and owes no homage to the sun?'

Five years after writing this, my father was happily married to my mother, and showing no inclination to associate with people she would have called cranks. He was still eating meat, and still attending his local Anglican Church. Allowing for his small town origins, he seemed almost normal. My grandfather would soon be doing something he would have thought wildly improbable a few years earlier – looking back with nostalgia on the time immediately after my parents had become man and wife.

# TWO

Because my parents were always loving towards me, it puzzled and upset me that they remained so cool to one another. It didn't seem fair that a reluctance to fight at the start of a war years ago, should be held against my father forever. But maybe there was something else I didn't know about? I found this possibility too alarming to think about it very often. One day, however, a significant discovery was thrust upon me.

At the end of a fine summer day in 1951, my father and I returned home after one of our long country hikes to be met by my mother at the door of the flat. Her eyes were brimming, even as the uniformed porter was closing the cage-like lift behind us. This was a worse reception than when my father had left my brand-new push-chair on a train. 'I'm amazed you didn't forget the boy too,' had been her reproachful comment then. Today, her cold voice scared me again. I hated to see her unhappy. She was normally such a cheerful, friendly person.

From behind the closed door of her bedroom, I heard my mother shout a woman's name, and I realized with a shock that I had met someone with that very name only hours ago on the slopes of Leith Hill. Just as we had come within sight of the tower on the summit, I had turned to look back at the view – and there she had been, tripping daintily from a copse to the right of the track, in a long spotted dress. Shortly after my father had introduced me to Joy Coley, I ran ahead on my own. She had made it very obvious that she was not pleased to see me with my father, and in any case I didn't want to go on hearing her whining at him in a miserable, breathless voice. It never occurred to me to try to listen to their conversation.

Even when I realized that my father had hurt my mother by seeing this person, I felt no anger towards him. I did not understand my mother's emotions and, even if I had done, I might still have thought him incapable of doing anything truly bad. As it was, I was bemused by all the fuss. It seemed so utterly unlike him *knowingly* to be causing my mother pain. In fact, I could not believe it of him and blotted the possibility from my mind. I would go on doing so for many years, helped by their politeness to one another in public.

When I was an adult, I learned that my father had first met Joy Coley in 1936, at the Kensington headquarters of the Order of the Cross, to which she too belonged. Joy's background was not remotely religious. She was the daughter of a big game hunter, Frederick Edgelow, who had prospected for gold in Rhodesia without much success, before moving to Bombay and becoming a barrister. He died when Joy was a child, as did her mother, so she was brought up in England by an aunt. Joy was just old enough to be a nurse during the final year of the Great War. Perhaps she was unsettled by it, for she did not remain long in any job afterwards, preferring to dabble at writing, and to read voraciously about religion. I know nothing about her husband, except that he was no longer living with her by the mid-1930s. Looking at photographs of Joy Coley fifty years on, I am surprised to see she was an attractive woman. My mother's many unflattering remarks have made me remember her only as she was in the 1960s – pale, ill-looking, with watery blue eyes. Mrs Coley – as my mother always referred to her with frosty politeness – became a serious threat to her happiness during the Second World War.

The war came at the worst possible time for my parents, creating fresh division just when their marriage was under pressure from my father's loyalty to the Order of the Cross, and his friendship with Mrs Coley. Given the military background of my mother's family – their motto was: *Pro Rege et Patria pugnans* (Fighting for King and Country) – she expected my father to enlist at once. When he confessed that his religious beliefs would oblige him to become a conscientious objector, my mother was mortified. Surely he could serve as a medical orderly? Not without being barred from the 'inner fellowship' of the Order of the Cross, he told her. All troops, whatever their function, were part of the same killing machine. My mother was torn between a husband who longed to be a pacifist, and a father who had been mentioned three times in despatches, and whose family had been riddled with admirals and generals for centuries. Feeling more sympathy for her father's point-of-view, my mother could not risk agreeing with him openly, in case she drove her husband into Mrs Coley's arms.

During the Blitz, my parents, my sister, Thomasina – then five years old – and my grandfather went to live just outside Gloucester, with my grandfather's elder daughter, Ierne, whose late husband, Major Claude Daubuz, had won the MC in the Great War. My mother must have felt more acutely than ever that my father was bringing shame on the family. All that summer he held out against her and her father. But in the autumn, he cracked unexpectedly, and agreed to serve in the army. He went to Shropshire for an officers' training course, but, Cranmer-like, recanted of his earlier recantation and, in January 1941, returned to Gloucester, once more refusing to consider military service of any kind.

Sir Thomas was not yet done, and initiated a lively debate. A graduate of Cambridge as well as Sandhurst, he was canny enough to emphasize altruism, rather than patriotism, as a reason for fighting: all tyrannies should be opposed in order to save whole populations from subjection. My father replied that few people who fought, even in so-called 'just' wars, were genuinely altruistic. Most took up arms out of fear of social ostracism, or to protect their privileges and possessions. Protecting the helpless was generally a very low priority. For religious people, he pointed out, there was a fate worse than losing one's life – putting one's immortal soul in danger.

My father tramped around Gloucester, praying in the cathedral, and seeking out Quakers and Unitarian ministers for guidance. In February 1941, he was summoned to appear before a conscientious objectors' tribunal in Bristol. Despite all his arguments, he was instructed by the judge to join the army for non-combatant duties. After a week of agonizing, my father chose, at the eleventh hour, not to oppose this order. Defending one's own country, he had finally decided, was not the same, in moral terms, as attacking somebody else's.

In August 1941 my grandfather tried to revive the idea of officers' training; but my father – by then a lowly lance-corporal in the Royal Army Ordnance Corps – was having none of it. He said he detested all string-pulling and had no desire to change his status. Living among ordinary people, he felt happier than he had done for years. In his diary, he quoted the Chinese philosopher, Laotse: 'He that humbles himself shall be preserved entire. He that bends shall be made straight.'

Living in camps in Hinckley, Worksop, Derby and Leeds, my father was happy to be removed from the tense atmosphere of home. With few responsibilities, he had time to attend lectures on art and literature, to go to concerts, and to walk for miles in the countryside. His diary gives a flavour of his varied leisure-time. In April 1942 he heard 'an inspiring talk' about the painter, Walter Sickert, and the following day he attended a vegetarian conference in Leeds. Next, he visited Fountains Abbey with a local stone mason. Delighted to be making friends with people from varied social backgrounds, he wrote: 'When aware of my sense of difference and privilege, I get a heightened desire to oppose all attitudes that deny equality.' In early May he bought a copy of the 'Bhagavadgita', which he promptly lost, and then replaced after rejecting the idea that his loss had been divinely intended. Indian mysticism became a life-long interest.

As my parents' relationship became more strained, they spent fewer and fewer weekends together in hotels and lodgings. Once, they stayed with my mother's aunt, Lady Noreen Bass, in a mansion in Staffordshire belonging to her husband, Sir William Bass, owner of the brewing millions. It's hard to fathom why my mother arranged this visit. Although Noreen was admirably supportive, introducing my father to everyone as her 'nephew', he felt absurdly out of place with his lance-corporal's stripe among the guests, who included a general and a colonel. That evening, my father noted primly in his diary: 'Had a talk on class and privilege with Norah. It became political at once, and therefore fruitless. The solution is not a political one. Nor can *man* solve it.' As usual, everything came back to God.

My mother ceased to visit my father after the summer of 1942. A year earlier they had stopped calling one another 'darling' or 'dearest' in their letters. My father's brand of mysticism was only open to people who gave up meat, abandoned ambition, read all the books by the Order's octogenarian founder, and set aside an hour a day for meditation. My mother instinctively mistrusted the mystic's aim of self-perfection, thinking it led to smugness. For a monk this might be reasonable, but not for a husband.

In August 1942, my father wrote in one of his notebooks: 'The union of man and woman is a cryptogram of the union of a soul with the One Life.' This symbolism baffled my mother. My father wrote reproving her for not trying 'to be one with him spiritually'. She replied:

> I *am* 'one with you' when we are together. It is natural and I love you very much then, as you are natural too and not full of (to me) difficult things. You are just a man and I am just a woman and we have each other and find pleasure and joy in our union. It's as it ought to be. I'm afraid I'm very near the earth – I love all the simple things: the smell after rain, good food, music, colour, books, the pleasure of the body, the blackbird in the garden singing.

Although my father also loved the beauties of nature, he felt unable to enjoy them with my mother. This was because she would not pretend to see nature as the physical manifestation of an unseen spiritual 'reality'. Life's purpose was a mystery to her, and she found his confident assertions on the subject unconvincing and embarrassing. My father *did* sometimes wonder whether his preoccupation with spiritual matters was too intense. He confided to his diary: 'Ideally, religion should just be a relaxed state of being.' But occasional moments of self-awareness didn't stop him meeting Joy Coley at the Order's summer school during the summer of 1943, nor did it prevent him becoming emotionally dependent. At about this time, Joy fell deeply in love with him. Only in sleep did my father's conscience seem to trouble him: 'A dream: with my hand in another's and my wife nearby. Her look of pain.'

In the autumn of 1943, my father joined the Airborne Division – an extraordinary decision, given his pacifist views of two years earlier. I suppose his transfer may have been due to my grandfather's clandestine machinations – or possibly his guilt over Mrs Coley made him want to do something conventionally martial as a form of reparation to my mother. Certainly, on commando raids, the line separating combat and support roles would blur to invisibility. Indeed, very soon he was being trained in the use of automatic weapons.

When D-Day came, my father was not part of the brigade chosen to capture Pegasus Bridge. But rumours of future missions disturbed my mother. She knew he was being put through exhaustive military preparations. A large-scale airborne drop on Germany seemed likely, soon. My mother decided the time had come to welcome him into her bed again, perhaps for the last time.

A week or two after my mother's resumption of conjugal relations, my father, still in England, was flying in a glider that crash-landed, hurting him and several other soldiers. The injuries to his back did not at first seem serious, but they would not respond to treatment. In mid-August, he was still in hospital in Harrogate, when to his amazement a medical board recommended his immediate discharge from the army. He would see the hand of God in this a month later, when most of the men he had trained with were captured or killed at Arnhem in the Netherlands.

Back in his dull job in the Aldwych – and feeling no more than occasional aches in his back – my father nodded off one afternoon and dreamed that a woman said to him: 'A child shall be born to you.' Since the Order's founder believed that the birth of Christ in the New Testament was an allegory for 'the birth of the Jesus life in everyman', rather than the birth of an actual child, my father was delighted. A spiritual birth within him seemed imminent. Unknown to him, my mother was pregnant, with me.

# THREE

About two weeks after swimming with my father in the men's pond in Hampstead, I went to the Eastman Dental Hospital for gum surgery, which I had been dreading. To my surprise, on entering the busy waiting room, I spotted my father sitting there. He beamed at me as I sat down beside him on a low plastic-covered bench. In front of us was a table heaped high with tattered magazines devoted to celebrity, dating, dieting, home improvement, and other matters entirely alien to him. These days, whenever I met him by chance anywhere, I couldn't quite believe I was seeing him. Perhaps this was partly due to some vestige of childish egotism (the kind which denies a parent independent life), but I think this was mainly due to the whimsical, will-o'-the-wispish quality that my father's inner preoccupations had always given him. In his crumpled grey, lightweight suit, with a book stuffed into a pocket, he looked like a member of another species among these waiting people in their brightly coloured shell-suits, trainers and T-shirts. But this visionary impression lasted only an instant. Of course, it *was* my father, and he had an excellent reason for being here. His new set of false teeth had hitherto defied the best efforts of ordinary dental technicians, and so were being fixed by the gods of this dental Valhalla. As I finished questioning him, he looked at me with sudden concern.

'I hope nothing very alarming brings you here?'

Even while I was telling him about my surgery, I was surprised to feel buoyed up by his soothing, sympathetic presence, just as I had when he'd sat beside my sick bed in childhood. I felt a little ashamed for letting him make *me* feel better, when *he* looked so disturbingly frail. I asked how he had got to the hospital and was horrified to be told 'on three buses'. I thought of his exhaustion on Hampstead Heath and begged him to catch a taxi home, which he promised to consider doing, though I knew he would return the way he had come. Then we talked of other things: his unpredictable brother's letters, my children's recent doings, and my book's progress, or lack of it.

Every time a name was called, I looked up, disappointed that it had not been mine. My father hardly seemed to notice that other people were being seen while he was not. This didn't surprise me. He had always been prepared to wait for hours without complaint. In the end, I was called before him, though he had been waiting longer.

As I was getting up, he produced some ripe plums from a stained paper bag. 'They're little beauties. Eat them later.' I slipped the fruit into a pocket, knowing I would probably squash them on my way home. He squeezed my hand. 'You'll be fine, Tim. We *both* will be.'

As I walked into the long oral surgery room, with its daunting rows of dentist's chairs, I suspected that my father had intended his last remark to allay my fears about his general health, rather than his dental problems. That he had done this so pointedly, made me feel uneasy all over again.

Once, when I was about eight years old, I walked into the kitchen and found my father seated at the table staring at a pile of my mother's bills. The door was immediately behind his chair, so he had heard, rather than seen me enter.

'Profligate woman!' he groaned, taking me for my mother.

In my parents' dictionary I found 'profligate' defined, not very helpfully, as: 'Recklessly prodigal, abandoned, extravagant, or profuse.' My father's anxiety over money may have increased my vocabulary, but it also distressed me. I have many memories of him avoiding spending on himself to compensate for my mother's excesses. Never catching taxis was one method, not owning a car was another, paying bills at the last moment was a third. When I was at Westminster School, he would bicycle to the school's bank, near Trafalgar Square, on the evening before term started, to thrust his cheque through the letter box. His habit of buying new clothes very infrequently was cost-effective only for a few years, since when everything wore out at last, more purchases had to be made than would have been needed if a full wardrobe had been judiciously rotated.

My father's unkempt appearance made my mother dread going with him to functions at my or my sister's school. Loving clothes herself, she never understood his indifference. But my mother had not read Kierkegaard's description of Jesus, underlined by my father in his copy of *Training in Christianity*, 'poor-looking, with no job, no prospects, and a desire to resemble humble people'.

My father's one indulgence was to purchase handmade leather shoes – an inconsistency for a vegetarian, but understandable, given his problems with his feet. My only memory of his ever losing his temper with me was in connection with a brand new pair of these shoes. He had taken delivery of them the day before, and was dissatisfied with the fit. Ignorant of this, I pulled off my sandals and placed my small feet in these gigantic leather boats, which I had found on the hall table next to a shoebox still containing crisp tissue paper. Cheerily, I clattered down the front steps and clomped around outside – until I heard his despairing roar. When he saw, through the open hall door, his chance of getting his money back vanishing down the garden path, he ran out after me. Thinking he was playing, I ran away from him into the street. The slap he gave me on the back of my legs, when he finally caught up, stupefied me. It would be several days before I would speak to him again.

In the early 1950s, my father wrote in a notebook:

> While still inhabiting the objective world, I will creatively secede from it, and from the tyranny of work, family and what others want me to be.

On reading this, I remembered his detachment, which resembled dreaminess more than inattention or boredom. My mother described his ability to cut himself off from all her demands as 'masterly inactivity'; and certainly he dodged with ease the barbs she aimed at his lack of initiative and ambition. In the same notebook, he wrote: 'The utter waster is more alive than the ambitious man because he does what attracts him, not what he feels he ought to do for advancement or esteem.' My father was fond of the sayings of Laotse and, in his copy of the Chinese sage's maxims, he had underlined: 'Attain complete vacuity and sedulously preserve a state of repose . . . Is it not by neglecting self-interest that one will be able to achieve it?' My mother had no time for provocative paradoxes. In her eyes, a man without ambition was failing his family and himself. Yet she stayed with my father.

Professor C. E. M. Joad – philosopher and regular Brains' Trust panellist – wrote at length in his autobiographical *Testament of Joad*, about a friend, whom he called 'C' – who though not my father, resembled him closely in many ways, and was, like him, a member of the Order of the Cross. Though Joad thought 'C's' beliefs incomprehensible, he described him as: 'A better man than any I had met – unselfish, good-tempered and serene. Whatever might happen to him, I felt he would retain his contentment.' It was the same with my father – even my mother acknowledged that, despite his shortcomings, he was an unusually good and humane man, and would sometimes say as much to me.

Above all my mother stayed with my father because my sister and I loved him, and because any break-up would have devastated us. But it would be naïve to imagine that her lack of money played no part in preserving the marriage. Sir Thomas had died in 1949, leaving her only a life interest in his estate – the capital being earmarked in his will for his nephew, the next baronet. (My grandfather had been under no compulsion to leave all his capital to his nephew, Rodney, for whom he felt little affection – considering schoolmastering to be no job for a future baronet.) Almost as distressing was my mother's discovery that her income would be much less than she had anticipated. To her amazement, her father's fortune had dwindled to a mere £15,000. A believer in his divine right to be rich, my grandfather had built a wing onto a house he had been renting, and, when younger, had owned racehorses and steeplechasers. My mother was also dismayed to discover that, after her mother's death, her father had kept an Italian mistress at the Savoy. She had not expected him to remain celibate, but the needless expense, coupled with her ignorance of it, wounded her deeply. Having inherited his title at the age of eighteen, my grandfather had never known a time when money had not been magically present. Inevitably, he had come to consider its plentiful supply a tribute to his rank, rather than to his readiness to limit the demands he put upon it.

In the meantime, my paternal grandfather, the man of trade, had died, leaving my father not exactly well-off, but, in a strange reversal of fortune, richer than my mother. Knowing my mother's gift for spending money, my father decided to send his inheritance abroad to be looked after by his only brother, who had gained a first at the London School of Economics before the war, and, in 1950, was working for the International Bank of Reconstruction and Development in Washington. My mother detested my uncle Ted, thinking him an eccentric and exceptionally self-satisfied man, so she deeply resented my father's decision. Since my uncle hated selling shares, his own and my father's, and my father could not bear to be berated as a spendthrift whenever he asked for any of his own money, his capital was effectively lost to him. After reluctant pleas, made by my father in exceptionally pressing circumstances, a few driblets would be returned – just enough to pay part of my sister's and my school fees.

By the time I was seven it was clear to me that my father disliked shops and shopping, and thought moral qualities, like modesty and unselfishness, the only possessions worth having. He always assumed that I was happier in the open air than 'stuck in some gloomy building full of things which no-one needs'. I'm afraid I played up to this view of me. In truth, I loved shopping with my mother and being bought presents. I'll never forget the bitterness of a female teacher at prep school on seeing my expensive Conway Stewart fountain pen and propelling pencil. ('It's disgusting to give a boy a beautiful writing set like that. I've got my knife into you now, young man.')

In the holidays, my mother took me to our local toy shop more often than was probably good for me – though, because the owner had lost half his face in the Battle of

Britain, my pleasure in choosing a toy was always mixed with pity and horror. Knowing that I would have been punished severely had I ever stared, I never got a good look at the astonishing pink patch covering the hole in the shop-keeper's face. Apart from banning staring, my mother was very strict about interrupting adults. To keep me quiet when she was entertaining, sometimes she seated me on a cushion in the corner. If I could be silent for ten minutes, I was told I would find, on standing up, that I had laid a pin. I must have been about five at the time, and it never occurred to me that she might have placed the pin in the cushion before I sat down. Instead, I was absurdly proud of my many successes.

My sister, Thomasina, had been cared for by a nanny from birth, but I was brought up by my mother. Before the war, she had depended on servants to do every domestic task, but after it, although she still had a resident Irish maid and a 'daily woman', my mother taught herself to cook and was surprised to find that she enjoyed feeding her family and shopping for us. At our local grocer's in the Earl's Court Road – then a dowdy and respectable street, little resembling the brash bedsitter-land it would become a decade later – customers sat on bentwood chairs while an assistant (my mother always waited to be served by the same middle-aged woman) fetched whatever was asked for, and someone else then parcelled up their purchases. My mother always bought the expensive coffee she had always enjoyed, the French wines, cheeses, *foie gras*, and everything else she was accustomed to, regardless of price. She never thought her buying habits extravagant – any more than she considered her frequent purchases of flowers for the house, presents for friends, and little items of china and jewellery for herself, as anything but necessities. She had no experience of balancing a budget, and would never adapt to the idea, however strongly my father commended it. She once told me, laughing wryly, that until 1940 she had assumed that everyone was given gas and electricity for nothing.

My mother loved jewellery and wore some treasured piece every day. So I knew when she sold items, it was from pressing need. In my teens I was once sent off to Bond Street to get estimates for a diamond brooch and a favourite pearl necklace. Also with money in mind, my mother took in, during my childhood, a succession of paying guests. All of these 'p.g.'s were girls in their late teens about to become debutantes and were marking time at secretarial colleges or finishing schools before finding suitable husbands. Their names were often memorable: Penelope Cave-Brown-Cave, Sue Twiston-Davies and Idonea Tudor, a cousin. My mother loved chatting to them and provided a lavish cooked breakfast and evening meal.

One afternoon, when I was six, I saw my mother ironing a lace-trimmed tablecloth, while Gracie, our maid, was polishing an ornate silver teapot and assorted water and cream jugs. 'Who's coming to tea?' I asked, hoping that this person would bring a child. Because my mother had been over forty when she had me, very few of her friends had young children.

'Lady Nosworthy.'

Brenda Nosworthy was another p.g., whose name I sometimes distorted into 'Noswhirly', but on this occasion, I simply asked: 'Why is Brenda's mother a lady?'

'Her husband was made a "sir" for doing something useful for the government.'

I considered this for a moment. 'Unlike grandpa who was a "sir" for doing nothing.'

'Old titles are just as good,' said my mother sharply. 'You know the old man in the hall?' I nodded, impatiently.

No-one could miss the huge portrait of a forbidding old man who looked like a pirate. 'He's grandpa's great-great-great-grandfather – the first admiral. Well, because his leg was shot off by a cannon ball at the Glorious First of June he was made a special kind of sir that could be handed down.'

'His leg came right off?' I was horrified. Before today, I'd known he'd been hit by a cannon ball, but not that his leg had been ripped right off.

'It didn't quite come off. The ship's surgeon had to finish the job with a saw. Then he was carried up to his quarter-deck in a cradle so he could see the rest of the battle. Mr Pitt – he was the Prime Minister – came down to Portsmouth and said he would be made a baronet.' Her tone was brisk and matter-of-fact.

I was still shaken. Why hadn't he screamed for a week, or longer, after losing his leg? In future, when I complained about a visit to the dentist, or having an injection at the doctor's, my mother would murmur sotto voce: 'Think of your ancestor.' I would repeat it to her years later when she had a hip replacement. Gracie said the admiral's portrait gave her the creeps, and I knew what she meant. His eyes were the kind that followed one wherever one went.

There were a couple of large prints of the battle in our dining room. One showed the fleet in the morning with all sails set, and the other was of the fleet in the evening, by which time many ships had been dismasted, and others were on fire or sinking. Men in the water clung to masts and spars, waiting to be rescued by small boats. I studied this picture closely and then made drawings of my own, adding various details like cannon balls in flight, and arms and legs lying on the deck.

On another occasion, my mother told me that her mother's surname, before marrying grandpa, had been Hastings, and that her ancestor, William, Lord Hastings, had been the king's Lord Chamberlain and his best friend. 'It was during the Wars of the Roses,' said my mother, making it all sound like a fairy tale. Suddenly, her voice became brusque: 'Then the king died and poor Hastings's head was chopped off.'

'Chopped off?' I echoed faintly.

My mother was already wishing she hadn't embarked on this piece of family history, but she couldn't take it back. She tried a sorrowful smile. 'I'm afraid that's how kings and great nobles punished their enemies . . . with an axe.'

'But had he done something really bad?'

'Quite the reverse. He tried to stop the dead king's brother, Duke Richard, from murdering the Princes in the Tower – they were the old king's children.'

'But that was good, wasn't it?' I hadn't got the hang of this at all.

'I know it was. But Richard wanted to be king himself and knew he couldn't be if the children stayed alive. So he decided to kill Hastings who would have tried to save them.'

'Did the children die too, mummy?' My eyes were brimming with tears.

'I'm afraid so.'

'That's so unfair.' I was crying aloud now.

'Tim, darling, I'm really sorry. But history isn't meant to be fair. It's just what happened years ago.'

'That makes it worse,' I choked. 'It shouldn't have happened. That's the whole point.'

This true story was scarier and nastier than the one about the admiral's leg. One moment Hastings had been walking about in his furs and fine clothes, being important and looking after the princes, and the next, a savage, unbelievable thing had been done to him when he wasn't expecting it.

Realizing she had upset me, my mother tried to soften the

blow by telling me that Hastings's grandson was made an earl to make up for what had happened, and that this reward for his family explained why four hundred years later my granny had been 'a lady from birth'. This was no comfort. My grandmother was long dead, but I was alive and soon having nightmares. On several nights, I dreamed that the head was lying on the ground with its eyes wide-open, staring at the spurting blood. When my mother next visited the butcher's, with me in tow, I blocked my ears so as not to hear the thump of the cleaver.

I learned to read at about this time. Leafing through the daily newspapers that were delivered to the house, I came upon a report of a man's death in a factory accident. He had been 'crushed to death in a machine'. Such a grisly death should have belonged only to the dead man and his family. But if written about for the world at large, surely it deserved a whole page and not just a few sentences crammed into a corner? I felt scared and shivery, and folded the paper at once, as if by doing so, I might keep this horrific event hidden away and not have to think about it. In the coming weeks, I would repeat this process whenever I came across anything similar in the papers – shutting away the horror that both fascinated and terrified me.

These frissons were already fading by the time I started to read history books for pleasure a year later. Soon after that, I stopped reading newspapers altogether. The violence of the Hundred Years' War made factory accidents seem tamer and less shocking. For one small boy, sitting in a shabby house in the wrong part of Kensington, tales of men in chain-mail, hacking each other to pieces with swords and axes, seemed more real than the milkman's horse clopping down the street outside. With history books to hand, and family heirlooms all around, I could draw medieval knights and Napoleonic soldiers for hours on end. I had to accept that my father had little interest in the kind of history I liked, and ignored most grim events in the newspapers, unless they involved cruelty to animals. My mother, on the other hand, was as fascinated by military history as I was.

I didn't care to admit it to myself, but I was starting to see my father in a more detached way by the time I turned eight. A year earlier, I had been delighted to earn his praise by telling some boys who'd been fishing on Wimbledon Common to throw their catch of minnows back in the water. Now, I blushed to think of this incident. My mother had told me about a quality called 'priggishness' and it was obvious to me now that this word had been invented for me. How could my father have let me slip into such a trap? Probably because he hadn't noticed I was in it. Not noticing, I was starting to realize, was quite a habit with him. He had recently taken up Chinese exercises, which he would perform in our back garden to the amazement of the boy next door. By now I was at Gibb's pre-prep school in Gloucester Road, and taking my first steps in conventional British manliness. Before I had started there, my mother told me (and not for the first time) that my father had done 'nothing worth talking about in the war'. I already knew from her that his reluctance to fight was something to be ashamed of. Looking back, it seems clear that my mother feared that unless I escaped my father's influence and acquired a little aggression at school, I would be sure to fail in life's Darwinian struggle.

When my father heard that there was to be a boxing competition at Gibb's, he took me aside after supper one evening. Although he appeared as calm as usual, I sensed that he was hiding the grief he really felt.

'About this boxing . . . You needn't think you have to hit other boys.'

'We do have to box, daddy.'

'If I talk to Mr Holding and say you don't like to hit people, I'm sure he won't try to make you.'

'A lot of boys will laugh at me if I sit at the side of the room.'

'It would certainly be braver not to box, than to join in with all the rest, knowing it's wrong.'

'I'm not brave, daddy.'

My father's disappointment made me long to promise not to fight. But just then my mother joined us, and I knew I would never say what he wanted to hear.

As if my mother wasn't there, my father said to me: 'Perhaps you'll find you *are* brave enough, when you think some more about it.'

'For God's sake!' exploded my mother. 'You can't seriously object to small boys boxing. They'll hardly be killing each other.'

'Just hurting and humiliating, and if he doesn't want to . . .'

As they began to argue, I left the room.

When the day of the competition arrived, I still toyed with the idea of refusing to fight, but, really, I knew I would box like all the others. When I told my mother this, her relief was obvious to me even at that age. I felt unworthy of my father, so I was thankful he would be at work and that only my mother would be coming to support me. Before the contests began, the headmaster told us boys, and our parents, that when the fights were over he would award two prizes: 'One for the best winner, and one for the best loser.' A ripple of laughter greeted this.

'You're laughing now,' he declared, 'but I promise nobody will laugh in a little while when I name the best loser.'

Aged seven and eight we could hit each other hard enough to black an eye, but not to knock each other out. The fight before mine ended with the loser sobbing loudly. No sooner out of my corner, I was driven back and pinned to the ropes by a succession of windmill sweeps from my taller opponent. Lacking the desire (and reach) to hurt him, all I hoped for was to come through the fight dry-eyed. My mother would hate it if I wept. So although my nose bled and my legs trembled, I showed no emotion. But as another blow to my face opened up my bottom lip, it was my mother's self-control that snapped.

'Hit him, Tim!' she screamed, above the hubbub. 'Just *do it!*'

As if invisible bonds had parted, I sprang forwards, punching wildly. This didn't happen till the last half-minute of the fight, but I still remember the glorious sense of permission, as I poured in my late flurry of blows. A roar of approval gave me an inkling who might soon be proclaimed the day's best loser.

Determined to preserve my prize forever, my mother would never cash the postal order I was awarded. Instead she paid me my winnings out of her own pocket. I never said anything about this to my father, but my mother must have made up for my reticence.

That evening, he said with an anxious frown: 'I hope you didn't feel you had to lose that fight.'

I shook my head vigorously. 'I did my best to win. Really.'

Though I guessed he didn't believe me, he squeezed my hand and said nothing more.

At Gibb's I first heard the word 'crank' and knew, without needing to be told, that my father was a prototypical specimen. The fathers of several of my school friends had won medals and crosses, and one, like the old admiral in the hall, had lost a leg. When asked by anyone about my father's war service I was evasive, except once, when I impressed the son of the legless hero by saying, in a sorrowful undertone, that,

44

although I hated to talk of it, my father's penis had been shot off. I had also discovered that besides winning crosses in the war, fathers were supposed to have been to the kind of schools *my* father had not attended.

By an excruciating twist of fate, it was the one-legged hero himself who asked me where my father had been educated. I had become friendly with his son, William, and so I was invited to his Holland Park home quite often. On that unforgettable day, as we were waiting for lunch to be brought in, William's father read out the report of a public school rackets match from his copy of *The Times*, as if these boys' antics were a matter of grave importance. The dreaded question of where my father had been to school came up later, while we were having tea. As I heard the hero articulate it, I felt a kind of deep thump in my chest, as if my heart had just compressed a dozen beats into one.

My grandfather had been to Marlborough, so I parroted the name of that famous school.

Legless was plainly delighted. 'That's a coincidence. I was at Marlborough myself.' As the floor seemed to drop away beneath me, I prayed that this was the worst moment and that the next few seconds would be better. I would be disappointed. 'I'll get the register of old boys,' he told me, happily. I watched him limp across the room and pluck a fat volume from a shelf. 'Everyone who ever went to Marlborough is listed in here.' As in a nightmare, I watched him start to turn the pages. 'I'll soon be able to tell you which house your father was in, and even which teams he played for.' I watched, and waited for my disgrace. A puzzled frown was already ruffling his brow. 'Did your father ever change his name, Timothy?'

'You could try looking under the name Chase,' I said, blushing fiercely as I plunged into yet another lie. 'Chase' was the surname of one of my parents' closest friends, who really had been to Marlborough, and who happened to be almost the same age as my father.

My tormentor found the entry at once and nodded approvingly. 'Here he is. Harry Fortescue Chase, born 10 November 1906. Do you know why your father changed his name?'

'Not really.'

'A while ago was it? Could have been due to a conditional legacy. Used to happen quite often before the war.'

Although I myself knew no-one who had changed his name, I could only surmise from the hero's satisfied expression that such people existed in reasonably large numbers. Now I would live in dread that Major Lancelot Glasson MC might one day meet my father, greet him as Harry, and try to swap anecdotes of their old school.

# FOUR

When my mother announced that she wanted me to go to a boarding school, I could not believe her. One reason for her decision may have been my increasing naughtiness. Whenever I visited the hero's son, William, we would either get into trouble, or narrowly escape it. Once, wearing our Harris tweed 'sports jackets' and corduroy trousers, we pushed a whole pyramid of deck chairs into the Round Pond. An elderly man, with an upright military bearing and a white moustache, spotted us and cried: 'You should be ashamed – boys of your class behaving like hooligans.' On another occasion, after changing the milk notes along one side of an entire street, we set fire to a pillar box, and, on returning home, doused a neighbour's gas-fire with a garden hose aimed through his window. The irate householder threatened to call the police and only spared us after insisting upon some humiliating grovelling. When William's mother briefly stopped us meeting, my mother got to hear about our misdeeds. Although she was very angry, I knew from what she said to my father, that she thought him to blame for never disciplining me.

Despite this, I told myself my mother loved me too much to send me to some distant country school. If it was 'the done thing' to go away, she would be tempted certainly, but with so many other boys at Gibb's going on to London day prep schools I felt reasonably safe. I was wrong. Only as an adult did it occur to me that her real reason was her desire to get me away from my father and to expose me to manlier and less cranky male role models. As she became more and more distanced from her husband, she seemed to be making the kind of choices her father would have advised if he were still alive. My mother was being cruel to be kind, or thought she was.

At no time can I remember my father resisting this plan, or even expressing regret – though, years later, my mother told me he had. Non-competitive himself, egalitarian, peaceable, unassuming, he allowed me to be sent away to a place where none of these virtues would be valued. In fact, it would be the school's unacknowledged purpose to eradicate all of them. Possibly, my father's belief that this world was only a shadow of the real one insulated him from distress.

During the term before I was due to go to East Sussex, my mother took me to Billings & Edmonds, the famous prep and public school outfitters in Hanover Square. Various items had to be ordered in advance, such as blazers (mine would be pink and have on its pocket a dolphin that looked like a slug). Possibly, she may have thought that if other boys were getting their outfits and trying them on in a cheerful and optimistic spirit, their attitude would infect me. Already I was resorting to superstitious rituals, avoiding walking on the cracks between the paving stones (if I miss a hundred cracks I won't be sent away) and praying in our local church. 'God, I'll become a vegetarian and give my pocket money to the poor if . . .' I made no appeal to my father, so he may even have thought I was happy to be going. But I couldn't see why he might want to help me when I had just chosen to box and to eat meat, and had shown no desire to meditate or follow his example in any way.

Boys who visited Billings & Edmonds were fascinated by the intricate model of Gulliver being pegged and corded to the ground by the Lilliputians; and I was no exception. But as I peered at it, I thought that it looked like a man being imprisoned by children. I had never heard of Dean Swift or Gulliver, so the model spoke to me simply as itself, and I knew that it was wrong. As I was being measured for my Sunday suit, it struck me what the model *should* be like: a small, childlike figure ought to be lying on the ground waiting to be tied up by lots of large grown-ups.

Although, to date, my mother had organized everything connected with my going away – including having an old trunk re-conditioned – for some reason of her own, she decided that my father should be the one to take me to see the school in advance. Perhaps she feared that if she were to see for herself the Spartan dormitories, the uncarpeted floors and drab changing rooms, she might not be able to face sending me anywhere so utterly unlike my home.

On a cloudless summer day in Coronation Year, 1953, my father and I travelled on the District Line to Charing Cross station. A few weeks earlier, I had seen *Tom Brown's School-days* on a neighbour's television, so I was understandably apprehensive. I had felt so upset by the film that I had not been able to face anyone afterwards, but had lain down on my bed for several hours. My father was just as he always was when planning a trip to the country: pleased by the prospect of a day in the open air and eager to make the most of it, although he must have known that this would be one of the last occasions on which I would accompany him anywhere as an innocent and uncritical companion.

Before we left, my mother urged my father to be sure to take a taxi to the school from Etchingham Station, and, above all, not to leave our sandwiches on the train. As we strode out of the country station into the shimmering heat haze, my father said it would be 'perfect folly not to walk on such a lovely day' and turned his back on the solitary cab in the station yard. A moment later, he patted his pockets with mounting agitation. The engine gave several deep, emphatic puffs as it began to pull the train's carriages towards Robertsbridge, along with our sandwiches.

My father had not thought to bring a map, so he was obliged to ask several villagers the way, then he turned to me, beaming. 'It'll only be a short walk.'

After about a mile, he admitted he had forgotten whether we ought to head for the school via Ticehurst or Hurst Green. So, inadvertently, he doubled what should have been a three mile journey. In a hamlet consisting of one small shop and a single row of tile-hung cottages, each with a flower-filled garden, he bought us a bottle of milk, a packet of biscuits and two apples. My mother had kitted me out in new sandals, and soon my right heel had been chafed raw by the stiff leather. Luckily, I was as used to blisters as I was to long walks, so I kept going after tying a grubby handkerchief round my foot. Although this did little to ease the pain, my worries about the school acted as an anaesthetic.

As on other walks, my father stopped here and there to rhapsodize about sights and smells: at first the dog-roses and wild honeysuckle in the hedgerows, then a hay field. Every-where, the luxuriance of new greenery delighted him. My father's enthusiasm could switch direction at a moment's notice – now fixing on a line of elm trees, now on an old wall, now a distant oast house. This didn't annoy me, since he was only behaving as he normally did when out walking – eager to share the pleasure he took in the world around him. And I think I may have found it comforting that he seemed so unconcerned about what we would find when we reached our destination.

My mother had told him firmly that he was not to wear one of his lightweight jackets because they crumpled so easily – luckily, I was too young to be concerned when I noticed that he was carrying just such a garment over his arm, with a book stuffed into a pocket. It was a hot day and his shirt was stained with sweat. When we sat down to rest in the long grass by the roadside, he read his book. Its name stuck in my mind – a horrible title: *The Sickness unto Death*. It was only in my late forties that I finally read Kierkegaard's most famous book.

And then at last, we were walking up a strange drive which would one day be numbingly familiar to me; looking up at a large prison-like building – mock-Jacobean, though I didn't know it; meeting the headmaster with his small steel-rimmed spectacles, pink cheeks and shining bald head; inspecting dormitories filled with iron-framed beds and uncurtained windows; visiting the 'hobbies room' and admiring balsawood aeroplanes and model warships.

The boys, in their grey shorts and aertex shirts, looked at me sideways or made a point of not looking at all. They didn't smile or speak. Some of them seemed to me to be almost grown-up, though thirteen was the leaving age. From the headmaster's study, I could see for miles across a wide valley. Closer to the school there were mown fields sloping towards shady woods. In one field, flatter than the rest, grey blobs were moving about slowly. These were boys playing cricket. At the centre of another field, closer to the house, was a distinctively shaped copse of fir trees. As I stared out at these dark firs, I could smell the headmaster's stale pipe-smoke and the resinous scent of pine logs. In a few months, I would associate both smells with the pain of being beaten.

In the changing rooms, a new scent: cricket bats steeped in linseed oil – a better smell by far than the odour of old food in the dining room, where a long sideboard was crowded with privately owned pots of Marmite, Bovril, Gentleman's Relish, and, in those days of continued rationing, a thin scattering of homemade jams.

All the time my father smiled benignly, asking questions about games, nodding to passing boys, commenting on the size and beauty of the copper beech flanking the front lawn, and never seeming to be anything but approving of this strange world with its scuffed lockers, cracked linoleum, peeling walls and ancient radiators. To him, we were all 'pieces of divinity in the making' and would have many lives before finally being perfected by the Father-Mother. Sometimes our suffering would be needed in order to test our faith and to help the whole process along.

After we had been given tea in the headmaster's sitting room, served by the headmaster's florid wife, we emerged on the gravel drive again. The headmaster looked about him with consternation.

'Your car? Where are you parked, Mr Jeal?'

My father favoured him with a smile I knew well: serene, otherworldly, vague.

'Car?' He raised his hands as if about to produce a rabbit from his sleeve. 'I'm afraid I don't have one.'

'Ah. You came by taxi.' The headmaster smiled briskly, already crunching across the gravel on his way to the telephone.

'We walked,' my father announced, quite loudly.

The headmaster spun round. 'Walked?' He seemed stunned.

'Not from London,' replied my father. I thought it a good joke but the headmaster didn't smile. I could feel myself blushing. Why could my father never lie? It was bad enough not having a car, but to admit to not having one, and then to confess to having walked rather than take a taxi was so embarrassing. Strangely, the headmaster's expression had changed from incredulity to respect.

'Do you know, you're the first visitors who've ever walked here from the station.' He looked at me more closely. 'Not bad for a boy your age.'

Moments ago I had hoped the ground would swallow me, but suddenly everything appeared to be all right. The headmaster took my father's arm and said we must be tired. Would we permit him to drive us to Etchingham Station? It seemed we had done something praiseworthy after all.

Soon, we were bowling along in his beige 'Ford Zephyr' in the free world again, where there were shops and pubs, and houses containing carpets and proper furniture and china, and where boys wore different coloured clothes, not just grey ones, and were not beaten on Wednesdays, and did not look away when strangers passed.

# FIVE

About a week after I had seen my father at the dental hospital, my mother telephoned with the news that he had been knocked off his bicycle in the Earl's Court Road. I had difficulty breathing.

'Is he badly hurt?'

'Only cuts and bruises and a broken wrist. He's in St Stephen's, Fulham. A juggernaut turned without seeing him and he nearly went under its wheels. He thinks it's a miracle.'

I went to see him that evening and found him sitting up in bed with one of his wrists in plaster and his other arm heavily bandaged. He admitted with a sigh that his cycling days were probably over. I could not help feeling hugely relieved. Only a week ago he had cycled back from some railway arches near London Bridge with two bulky sacks of sawdust (a cheaper substitute for cat litter) tied to his handlebars, and another sack strapped to his back. My mother had been horrified, and not only by the danger he had been in.

'He looked exactly like a refugee with all his possessions tied to his body.'

Thinking about the accident, it amazed me that my father had not had one years ago. Ever since I could remember, he had been absent-minded. At the start of a family holiday when I was five, he managed to lose all our tickets within ten minutes of getting on the train. I've never forgotten the tone in which my mother said, 'Oh, Joe!' Her voice despairing, incredulous, and yet almost awed. There had been the dinner jacket he left behind on a tube train less than an hour after hiring it from Moss Bross. (His own dinner jacket he had given away years ago as a gesture aimed at my grandfather, who had often dressed for dinner.) When I was fifteen and she twenty-five, my sister vowed never again to be driven by our father – so often had he ignored the road, in favour of the sights beside it. We had come closest to death on our way to our aunt's funeral, the almost fatal attraction being an ancient mulberry tree in a Hampshire garden. My father had a passion for mulberries.

The purpose of the cycle ride that had landed my father in hospital had been to take a flask of soup to Mrs Coley. That my mother should let him give away soup, which she had made, to the woman who had once caused her so much pain, struck me as curious. I could only suppose it gave her a sense of power over this woman my father had never truly broken with. And there would have been the bonus of a most satisfying irony: the soup itself was made with veal bones. So my vegetarian father and his vegetarian girlfriend would sit drinking this thick broth together, having no idea what was in it. (It had been forty years since either had knowingly eaten meat, so they had long since forgotten its taste.) This soup really was extraordinarily meaty, and, on becoming cold, a skin of fat formed on the top. When I realized that my mother was serving my father the very soup I had imagined her making solely for her guests, I said:

'I think you're doing something really wrong.'

'Do you, indeed?' she demanded, not in the least shame-faced. 'Do you have any idea how hard it is to feed him day after day when he won't eat fish, and can't be given cheese or eggs every meal?'

For her, his diet was nonsense, like his religion, and my intervention was presumptuous meddling. In future, out of my sight, I guessed my father would be given other meaty soups after returning from work. I believe she thought she was doing him good.

On the next occasion when I went to have dinner with my parents, my mother led me into the kitchen and actually lifted a bone from the pan. She then gave me an audacious stare, as if daring me to tell him. Without doubt, I was being punished. She seemed to know I wouldn't create a scene. It depressed me to have to admit that her confidence in my cowardice was well-placed.

In the dining room, minutes later, with a steaming soup plate in front of each of us, I hardly knew where to look. When my father took a first sip and said in his slow, slightly husky voice: 'No-one makes a vegetable soup like you, Norah,' and moments later added: 'You've really excelled yourself with this one,' I didn't know how to contain myself.

About two or three times a year, when I was in my teens, my mother and I visited the Hurlingham Club together. I was a keen tennis player and I went there fairly often by myself to play with friends. One Saturday in June 1960, my mother and I had tea outside the house and listened to the resident Palm Court trio, before watching the cricket. The memorably named Stragglers of Asia were playing a team I can't remember. My mother had no interest in cricket, so most of her energies went into talking to me. After inquiring about my impending confirmation, she turned the conversation to reincarnation, and asked what I thought of it.

'I *don't* think of it,' I replied, recognizing an attempt to manoeuvre me into laughing at my father's beliefs.

'Not at all?' Eyebrows raised in incredulity. 'Though your father thinks he may come back as a bug or a budgerigar?'

'He doesn't think that.'

'He expects to be the Dalai Lama, next time, does he?'

Somehow I managed not to smile. I didn't blame my mother for feeling exasperated with my father for giving more time to his spiritual search than to her, but I still would feel guilty if I ever played her game. Some decorous clapping greeted a boundary. My mother had brought her teacup with her and she drained it with satisfaction, before treating me to a winning smile.

'Forget about him. Just think of little me, with my false hip, etcetera. If I'm put into the body of a tall Red Indian after I die, how can I be the same person I was in this life?'

'Your *soul* will be in the Red Indian, not *you*.'

'What good will it do me if my soul's inside someone else and I don't know about it?'

'I haven't the foggiest. We did a "topic" at school on life after death, and someone said reincarnation was like leaving a tube station and stopping at another station after a dark tunnel.'

'I suppose we have no memory of the earlier station?'

'So?'

'You're sure it wasn't your idea, Tim?' She was gazing at me knowingly.

'It wasn't.'

'I'm glad about that, because it's a damned silly one. Life's nothing like a station. Even if it was, you'd be a different person each time you stopped anywhere.'

Suddenly the fielders were animated. A batsman had been caught behind. Applause rippled around the ground as the players began to amble towards the big copper beech near the corner of the house. The Stragglers' innings was over. Rather than wait for the other side to bat, my mother suggested watching the croquet.

Passing the classical portico of the house, she said in a completely sincere voice:

'One day we'll die, and suddenly we'll be somewhere else, or we'll be nowhere at all. Till then we shouldn't pretend to know anything about it.'

Soon we were watching middle-aged people in white flannels playing croquet in a leisurely, Edwardian way. I felt bored at once. Even children's tennis would have entertained me more.

'Such a fiendish game,' said my mother, sinking down contentedly into a deck chair. 'I played a lot when I was a child and loved it. You would too.' She smiled affectionately, and I found myself smiling back.

A fortnight after my father's discharge from hospital, he and my mother came to dinner at my house. Getting out of the taxi – the first he had taken for several years – my father stumbled. I told myself that his shakiness was due to his accident. His sling wouldn't be helping his sense of balance either. After we had eaten, he told me that he hadn't yet managed to finish his income tax return, and with his right hand in its present condition, wouldn't be able to do so for a while. Would I be willing to help? Assuming I would, he introduced me to the contents of a bulging envelope.

His current tax return turned out to be almost identical to those he had made in previous years. Since he had already listed his dividends, pensions and so forth – and my mother's trust income was well documented by the solicitor to her father's estate – the job took me little more than an hour. All I then had to do was add up everything and make a fair copy.

Before completing my task, I became puzzled by my father's handwriting. Why was it so small, and why did it slope downwards at the end of lines as if trying to tumble from the page? His notes and figures for earlier years did not slope and were hardly cramped at all. The change seemed to have happened gradually, which made me suspect his eyesight was to blame. A couple of years ago, my father had abandoned his Bates exercises and had got himself a pair of reading glasses, after years of holding books at arms' length and blaming the size of the print for his difficulties. Now, maybe he needed a stronger pair.

I mentioned this possibility three weeks later, while taking him to buy a jacket and a pair of trousers in Camden High Street at Alfred Kemp's – a shop he had spotted from a bus, with no great difficulty since the words SECOND HAND CLOTHES and ALFRED KEMP WILL FIT ANYONE stretched across the whole building above the shop in letters ten feet high. At once, my father became offhand and unco-operative. Assuming this was because a new pair of spectacles would bring unlooked for expense, I did not press him. Yet there was something disturbing about this whole business. In other years he had completed his tax return within a month of the end of the preceding fiscal year. This time he had left an interval of five months before doing anything. But more immediate matters occupied me. His wrist was only just out of plaster, and he needed help trying on trousers.

'At home, I do this sort of thing sitting down.'

'Even though you've got your hand back again?'

'Don't you start. Norah's always on at me for being slow.'

I was finding it surprisingly hard work assisting him, so I understood what she meant. His sense of balance had not returned after his accident, and I often had to prop him up. Helping him with some recalcitrant fly-buttons – he had always hated zips – I almost let him fall. He was characteristically forgiving, although I had given him a nasty shock. The staff had been nowhere to be seen at the moment of crisis. In general, they adopted a lordly attitude towards all of their customers in this cornucopia of cast-offs.

I watched my father examining yet more trousers. Had it occurred to him that most of these items had once belonged to people no longer living? What a crowd there would be if all the owners returned to reclaim their clothes. An ideal subject for a large Stanley Spencer painting, although much bleaker than the *Cookham Resurrection*. To my mind, dead men's clothes always suggested stand-ins for the garments section of a Holocaust museum.

Choosing a coat proved easier, and soon my father was delighted with a lightweight jacket in a vigorous check. I guessed that my mother would say it made him look like a bookie, and later she did. She was never able to come to terms with his shopping habits. But, as I pointed out, he was most unlikely, in Alfred Kemp's, to bump into anyone she knew.

'It's not *that*,' she groaned, 'it's the *idea* of the previous owners.'

Of course I knew what she meant, though my father would have been baffled. What could be wrong with other people and their clothes? They were all children of God. Even his father-in-law had been that, despite his constant disapproval, and my father may have found this thought reassuring, when wearing Sir Thomas's overcoat – which he did for almost twenty years after my grandfather's death.

Not long after my father's cycling accident, my mother felt alarmed enough by his slowness to telephone the doctor.

Even simple tasks, like fastening buttons and washing up, were taking my father ages. In late September, my mother told me that he had sat for hours at a time, day after day, before deciding to ask me to help with his tax affairs.

'I wish you'd told me sooner.'

'I didn't want to worry you. But he's got much worse. Sometimes, he freezes up entirely.'

She was worried, but irritated too, perhaps believing that his immobility might be due to a lifetime of indecision. 'Pick up your feet,' I would hear her groan, as though to counter an unresisting decline into senility. Yet his distress finally persuaded her to seek help.

Within a month of her telephone call to the doctor, my father was seen by a neurologist at University College Hospital and underwent tests. A week later he was given the results in person at the hospital. That afternoon he came up to Hampstead to see me.

We walked out onto the small area of the Heath near my house, known as 'Preacher's Mount'. There, under the trees, my father broke it to me that for several years – maybe as many as five – he had been suffering from Parkinson's disease. His shuffling gait and cramped writing were classic symptoms, apparently. Far from surrendering prematurely, he had been battling for years against an insidious illness. I put an arm round him, numbed by his news. I'd heard that the disease was progressive and incurable, so he probably knew this too.

It was an exceptionally beautiful autumn afternoon with the sun glowing golden through the mist. Everywhere the leaves were turning. Even today, my father appeared to be enjoying the natural scene.

He said: 'God sends us nothing we can't endure.'

I knew he had meant this reassuringly, but it made me feel

worse. 'How could a loving God have sent you such an awful disease?'

'To bring me to Him.' A faint smile. 'Which may be why I have the disease and not you. He knows *I* will come to Him.'

'How does he know?'

'Because years ago I came very close. He's making sure I need His help badly enough to turn to Him again. It's my second chance.'

I took his arm as we crossed East Heath Road to the main Heath. I was distressed to find I knew so little about the beliefs which mattered most to him.

In the Lime Avenue, he stopped to admire the sunlight as it filtered downwards in misty columns. When he wanted to get moving again, he found he couldn't, and it took him almost a minute to take his next step. When he was walking again, I was scared that his next involuntary pause might last even longer. As if unaffected by what had just happened, he asked: 'Did you ever read any of John Donne's sermons?'

'Perhaps years ago.'

'Read them again. In one, he tells how God had just failed to get into him by His normal channels: speaking to him, blessing him, and so forth; so, instead – this is what Donne says – "God shook my body with agues, set it on fire with fever, and frightened the Master of the house, my soul, with such horrors, that at last He made an entry into me."'

'All God had to do was whisper to you.'

'You're wrong. I never yielded up my selfish will.'

How typical of my father, I thought, to deny himself the credit even of his self-effacement. I said: 'What happens to people who *do* succeed in giving up their will?'

'They're able to love their neighbours, trust in God's goodness, and very soon . . . You don't look happy, Tim.'

How could I, while watching him negotiate his way so gingerly between the stones on the path? I was overwhelmed by the ridiculous unfairness of his illness. Why him of all people? 'I'm fine,' I said. 'Please go on.'

'Then, when they're living naturally in Christ's way, or Krishna's, which is as good, they'll find they're able to withdraw from their bodily senses and the world around them, and rise to a level of consciousness where they can experience union with the Divine.'

Because his words were nebulous to me, and unconvincing in the way religious phrases usually seemed to be, I simply nodded. My father favoured me with the patient, good-humoured look he usually reserved for openly sceptical responses. His religious certainty made me fear for him. What if his faith failed him as his illness grew worse?

We sat on a bench beside the playing field. It was mid-week, and there were no boys kicking footballs, and only a few dog-walkers about. How many more times would we be able to sit here together?

He said quietly: 'My illness is part of God's purpose for me. Nothing arrives by chance.'

'You mean it was predetermined?' I was appalled that he should think this.

'My own actions affect the outcome too.' He placed a hand on mine. 'Only by being brought to the point of despair can we be perfected. Read Kierkegaard. Suffering helps us to love others.' My father's voice had become softer and less distinct. 'We reach God when he's improved us.'

'I hate the idea of "necessary" suffering.'

'It's hardly new. Christ invites us to take up our crosses for our own good. "I am the Way . . ."'

Returning along the Lime Avenue, my father's shuffling progress was slow but sure.

'They're going to treat me with a powerful drug. Part of my brain isn't producing a substance that's needed for communication between brain cells. There's only this one form of treatment.' He grinned at me. 'Lucky I'm not a Christian Scientist.'

We trudged on in silence as the sky turned a deeper red – a phenomenon caused by dust in the atmosphere. How could my father believe that the all-powerful creator of the limitless universe had taken the trouble to invent a complex system of atonement for the microscopic beings on a single star? But what did I know about it all? Maybe God really was the unifying consciousness of the universe, and our minds were individual cells in His massive brain – divine without our knowing. As we came to East Heath Road again, I reached for my father's arm, but he insisted on crossing without my help.

On the pavement outside my house, before I drove my father home, he showed my eldest daughter, Jessica, the way he had been taught to walk by a physiotherapist at the hospital: back straight, heels meeting the ground firmly, arms swinging.

Jessica, then seven, laughed delightedly.

'Grandpa's a soldier. Look!' And she too swung her arms.

My father continued up the street for her benefit, marching as if to the beat of a distant drum.

# SIX

One evening in the summer of 1956, when I was on holiday from prep school, my father suddenly called me to the sitting room window of our house in Earl's Court Gardens.

'Come quickly.' His tone was so urgent that I tossed aside *Popski's Private Army* and hurried to the window. Pulling back the net curtain, he gestured across the street to where an elderly man in a grey suit was paying off a taxi. For some reason (obscure to me), my father was ecstatic. 'By jiminy,' he chuckled, 'it's not every day one sees the world's most famous poet coming to see his girlfriend.'

'What's his name?' I asked, suspiciously. Was my father having some kind of quiet joke at my expense?

'T. S. Eliot.'

I'd heard of him, but only just, so I could hardly share my father's enthusiasm. The tall and gangling poet finished paying the driver, and walked down the steps into the basement of the house opposite. And that was that.

'Is he going to see the red-haired woman?'

'You mean Valerie Fletcher. He most certainly is.' My father was delighted to be sharing this poignant moment with me. He liked Valerie and evidently saw nothing reprehensible in the age gap between her and this elderly beanpole.

Next door to the house in which Miss Fletcher rented rooms was a taller building, which, like hers, backed on to the District Line railway track. For about four years this had been a drinking club, 'The Tilted Glass'. Since members often vomited or urinated in our front garden on leaving, my father was organizing a campaign to get it closed down. This had led to meetings with other residents, including Valerie Fletcher and her landlady, Miss Harris, whose long tobacco-stained teeth enthralled me whenever we met in the street.

In the days when Mr Eliot called on Miss Fletcher in Earl's Court Gardens, she was his secretary at Faber & Faber, where he was a director. I remember the future Mrs T. S. Eliot coming to dinner with my parents on several occasions, although I can't recall anything she said. One day my father told me that he had met Mr Eliot at Miss Harris's and had talked to him about 'A. E.' Russell's mystical poetry and Yeats's early poems. Having no sense of his own importance, or lack of it, my father was unabashed by fame, however great. Genius, he believed, had divine origins, so contact with any possessor of it was wholly pleasurable. Convinced that his conversation had gone well, my father suggested, when next they met, that Mr Eliot would be the ideal person to edit an anthology of mystical verse. Although this idea seems to have been received without obvious enthusiasm, my father, ever the optimist, continued to think 'something would come of it'. In the end it did – but not what my father had had in mind.

In 1962, over five years after Miss Fletcher became Mrs Eliot, I became co-editor of my house magazine at Westminster. Soon after my appointment, my father horrified me by suggesting that I ask Mr Eliot for an interview. Didn't he understand that it wasn't even the school magazine? I had read somewhere that Mr Eliot valued his privacy more than anything (Mrs Eliot apart) and hardly ever gave interviews to publications of any kind.

'But don't you see, Tim, that gives you a far better chance? He'll be amused to be asked by a schoolboy.'

I was seventeen now and well aware of T. S. Eliot's unique fame. Imagining him seeing, in the magazine's pages, snippets about house sport and other trivia jostling with his fine words, I wanted to forget the idea. But my father would not be discouraged. I should be sure to mention in my letter, he told me, the fact that my home was opposite Miss Harris's house, where I had once seen Mr Eliot arrive by taxi; and I should add that my parents had known his future wife when she was Miss Fletcher. I thought all this was poor advice. Why would Mr Eliot be swayed by the coincidence of my living opposite? Because, said my father, everything was part of a great plan, in which, strictly speaking, there were no coincidences. Besides, every imaginative person enjoyed a surprise now and then, however busy he or she might be.

In the end I wrote a letter along the lines my father had suggested. Several weeks later, Mr Eliot had still not replied. I wasn't really disappointed for myself, but I did feel sad for my father. But just when I was about to break the bad news, the poet's answer arrived. Mr Eliot agreed to be interviewed at Faber & Faber, and suggested a time during the afternoon of 16 May. This was just over a month away. He ended his letter: 'My wife has reminded me that your parents were very kind to her some years ago, when she lived across the street from them.' On being shown the letter, my father forbore to say he'd told me so.

I was extremely nervous as I arrived in Russell Square for the interview, but I took comfort from my co-editor's presence and that of the headmaster's secretary, who I hoped would take down an accurate shorthand account of the interview. Our questions were on popular as well as poetic subjects, and in answering even the most predictable of them, Mr Eliot said pithy and memorable things. I was surprised to find that I enjoyed the whole experience in a dazed and pinch-me kind of way.

*The Manchester Guardian* obtained a copy of the magazine soon after its publication, and the short piece which appeared in that paper, gives a flavour of the interview itself:

### Schoolboy enterprise

Where has T. S. Eliot stated that he admires very much Peter Sellers's work in 'I'm All Right Jack'? Why in the *Grantite Review*, of course. This is a magazine enterprisingly put out by the boys of a single house of Westminster School. Mr Eliot has granted them an interview taking up five quarto pages, and not a line of it is condescending or facile. There are careful answers to questions such as: 'Do you feel that a period of doubt is essential to the gaining of faith?' And some good epigrams: 'Richard III is a pure villain, and pure villainy is one kind of purity in which it is difficult to believe. Even the devil is a fallen angel.' Again, about the publication of Rose Macaulay's letters: 'One cannot always read books just to decide whether they ought to be read or not.'

But this is to leap ahead. The interview's genesis was painful. In the first place, the original draft, which I had sent back to Mr Eliot had been full of mistakes and misquotations which he had been very kind about – re-shaping the entire interview for us, without making us feel too ignorant. Worse embarrassment lay ahead. Although the proofs were read by my English master and my housemaster – and not just by me and another boy – when the finished copies were delivered early one evening in June, my stomach turned over.

An appalling misprint leapt out at me almost as I plucked the first copy from the box. Where 'The Waste Land' should have appeared in the text, some wag at the printer's had substituted 'The Washstand'. I stared at the terrible error for almost a minute, as if by sheer concentration I might make it vanish. Praying that this was a rogue copy, I flicked through several others, only to encounter it again and again. My triumph now seemed destined to make me a laughing stock throughout the school.

When I was calm enough to trust my legs, I ran to the nearest telephone and rang my father, who, mercifully, had just got in from work.

'What can I do?' I gasped, close to tears. 'We can't reprint them all.'

'There's only one thing to do,' he said serenely. 'You must go and see Mr Eliot and tell him what's happened. He'll know what should be done. Has he given you his home phone number?'

'Yes. But what can I say to him?'

'That the printers have made a mistake which you'd like to show him. Offer to take a copy to his flat this evening. Get a taxi if he's at home.'

Because I was a weekly boarder, I needed my house-master's permission to break bounds after six; but he agreed at once that I should telephone Mr Eliot and, if possible, see him. And so I spoke to the great poet on the telephone, describing the printer's mistake in vague, face-saving terms. I must have sounded wretched because he decided to end my misery at short notice. Within half-an-hour, at Mr Eliot's invitation, I was rattling through Kensington Square in a taxi, and drawing up outside his ground-floor mansion flat.

I remember nothing of the flat or my arrival – only that Valerie Eliot opened the door, and that I was soon babbling my apologies about 'The Washstand'. When I stopped speaking, he looked at me impassively through his spectacles, stooping slightly towards me. Whether he was angry or upset, I had no idea. His face remained expressionless. Yet I realized he was suppressing strongly felt emotion – possibly anger. And then – this was terrible – he seemed to be gasping for breath, a strange wheezing, choking sound, that only after several seconds became recognizable as laughter. He laughed until his eyes were overflowing and until he was obliged to sit down. My own eyes filled with tears too – tears of relief.

Before leaving, I promised to print *erratum* slips and paste them over every 'Washstand'. Mr Eliot thought this would be best for much of the edition, but he asked me to make no corrections to his own two dozen complimentary copies. There were, he told me, numerous collectors of everything he wrote, not just editions of his poetry, but of his essays, interviews and lectures, and these people were 'as crazy as stamp collectors'. A 'real howler' like 'The Washstand' would be especially prized by them – the more so for being in a magazine with a restricted printing.

'All's well that ends well,' said my father when I rang him later that evening. Though pleased, he was unsurprised by Mr Eliot's reaction. He had known from the beginning that the man of genius would not disappoint him.

# SEVEN

Remembering how grim most boarding prep schools were in the 1950s, in retrospect it seems strange that more parents didn't remove their children. In fairness to my mother, she only realized towards the end of my time in East Sussex that I had never settled in all my five years. One reason for her ignorance was the school's censorship of letters. On my first Sunday, as on all subsequent ones, the whole school spent a supervised hour writing home. Being innocent of the *mores* of the society I had just entered, I told my mother I felt homesick at night, and also longed to be with her in the day. I sealed up the envelope, assuming that what I had written was private. An hour later, the headmaster's wife cornered me in the changing room and pointed out that boys' letters should never be sealed until approved. This, she told me, was a precaution 'in case boys wrote home selfishly and distressed their parents'.

She bent so close to me that I could see the broken veins in her cheeks. 'Isn't that what you have just done, Timothy? Wouldn't it be kinder and braver to tell your parents you felt homesick at first, but are better now? Add colour to your letter by telling them about carpentry and rugger.' She then tore up my first effort.

Schools like Boarzell seemed to be preparing boys for a harsh life on the frontiers of an Empire, which, by 1953, was doomed. Soon I took on, as my own opinion, the regulation view that boys who complained about physical hardships, such as cold showers in February, and playing rugby on frozen pitches, were contemptible. Even before I came to this conclusion, my letters home had needed no vetting. Only recent new boys tried to express what they felt, rather than what they soon knew they ought to feel. It was strange how we added rules of our own to an already rules-bound existence. Our prohibition on 'sneaking' to a master about bullying, or thieving from tuck boxes, might have enabled us to hold out in a German prison camp without betraying the location of an escape tunnel, but in the 1950s it merely meant that our daily lives were much nastier than they need have been.

Our schoolboy code could even oblige a boy to let himself be beaten for a crime he had not committed. Once, a master overheard a member of my dormitory saying that I had poured a mixture of toothpaste and hair oil down another boy's throat to stop him snoring. Although someone else had done this, I could only have escaped punishment by naming him. I found it easier 'to take my beating' than earn months of unpopularity by giving him away. I loathed corporal punishment, yet felt no animosity towards our pink-faced, bespectacled headmaster, viewing him more as a malign force of nature than as an ordinary human being who could have behaved differently, if he had wished.

The most ludicrous beating I ever received was the result of a letter I wrote to Weston's Biscuits, asking for free samples. Instead of sending me the hoped-for box or packet of biscuits, the firm's regional sales manager instructed his nearest representative to visit the school when next in the area, on the reasonable assumption that T. Jeal Esq. was a master, with power to place orders. My clandestine use of matron's typewriter had strengthened this illusion. The headmaster justified his decision to beat me on the grounds that I had tried to obtain free goods by deception, which was 'little better than theft'.

I never mentioned to my parents the mauve and purple bruises that dappled my buttocks in term time and which earned me admiring comments in the showers. My fear of being guilty of unmanly whingeing only partly explains my reticence. I may have feared that my parents' sympathy would pierce the defensive hide I was trying to grow. Worse still, if I told them how I really felt, and they failed to remove me, how would I be able to think they still loved me?

So when my parents came twice a term to take me out –

invariably in a tiny hired Austin A35 – I would rarely say anything to raise the emotional temperature, even when the time for parting approached and sadness pressed in on me like a fog. Until then, I was always overjoyed to be with my parents. Usually I invited a friend to come with me, and the presence of this extra boy ruled out honest talk and led to much light-hearted chatter. Perhaps my mother went home delighted by her choice of school. My father gave no clue to his thoughts. Maybe the unfamiliar experience of driving his wife and several boys around the countryside fully engaged him – although from time to time he would point out landmarks, like Rudyard Kipling's house, or he would make admiring comments about a group of trees or a bull in a field.

Anything could be endured if treated as routine, even hearing through the closed door of the headmaster's study the thwack of a leather-heeled slipper connecting with the buttocks of the boy ahead of one in the weekly punishment line. Afterwards, with flesh on fire, I would race to the nearest dormitory and leap from bed to bed, swearing aloud until the pain became manageable. And why was I being 'made a man' at this particular place? Because my godmother – a Miss Catherine Holt, whose grandfather had founded the Blue Funnel Line, later the Ocean Steamship Company – was distantly related to the headmaster and had become the school's largest benefactor. *That* had been reason enough for my mother to send me here.

Our Spartan life was not entirely without compensations: such as the huts we built in the woods, the wild strawberries we picked, and the friendships we formed. One of my friends, with whom I played chess, was the son of the domestic chaplain to the Archbishop of Canterbury, and I was excited to be invited to Lambeth Palace during the holidays. On returning home, my father questioned me eagerly. Had I met His Grace? And what had he said? And what buildings had I been shown? The Archbishop's private chapel or the Lollard's Tower? I could hardly tell him that we had spent most of the time in a potting shed at the end of a sunburned lawn, being taught to inhale Woodbines by the gardener's son, who blew smoke down his nose, and, as an encore, produced his erect penis for our edification. I stared in amazement. 'Never seen a knob before?' Being too young to compete, we could only marvel at his colossus.

Back in rural Sussex, small acts of vandalism, born of anger and rebelliousness, enlivened our days. A boy, regularly picked on by a master, took all the football socks from the changing room lockers and thrust them into the furnace, before running away. He was found in Hastings by the police and was brought back in a black Wolseley with a bell. To stop him becoming a hero, he was expelled.

Boys who committed crimes, and did not come clean, were blackmailed into confessing. The headmaster summoned the whole school to the sixth form and declared that unless the boy, who had for instance crept into the kitchen and poured ink into the porridge, had confessed by noon, the whole school would be kept in detention on Sunday afternoon. Since this was the only free afternoon of the week, immense pressure would be put on the ink-pourer to give himself up. I myself was once in this position, after a friend and I had committed what was later described as the worst crime in the school's history – though I doubt whether it really was.

Why did a friend and I decide, aged twelve, to write an obscene letter to the sister of a boy in our class? We had never met the girl, and did not dislike her brother, but, for some unfathomable reason, we still chose to forge his hand-

writing, making it appear that he found his sister so physically loathsome that he hated coming home for the holidays. While copying his writing from his History exercise book in preparation for our forgery, we imagined this unknown girl opening the letter and starting to howl. Pretending to be her, we flung ourselves about choking and wailing, before collapsing in fits of laughter.

The process of the forgery involved reproducing a large number of words and individual letters of the alphabet on tracing paper, and then rubbing a soft pencil over the back. By pressing through the see-through paper onto a chosen sheet of Basildon Bond, I assembled whole sentences, word by word, letter by letter, in the brother's hand. Once I had produced a satisfactory pencil version of the entire letter on a sheet of writing paper, I wrote over the pencilled letters in ink and then rubbed the paper clean of pencil marks with a ball of bread – the softest kind of rubber. The end result looked uncannily like our classmate's handwriting. And what predictable words had we chosen with the help of Len, the fifteen-year-old son of the school cook? 'Prick', 'cunt' and 'spunk' of course, along with other jewels from his enviably specialized vocabulary.

Although the forged script was impressive, the content of our letter was infantile. Not even a deranged brother would have written in such terms to his sister. He thought her face looked like 'her pony's cunt', we had him tell her, along with other smut. Puerile though our letter was, it had still carried a knock-out punch in 1957. I had never heard the word 'cunt' until Len had whispered it to me, with a self-satisfied smirk, in the deserted pantry one evening after prayers.

Our letter could not be risked in the usual box on the stationery cupboard. So I slipped through the gates after games and posted it in the pillar-box on the Ticehurst road. As the postman carried it to its target, what did we hope for? Not that the girl's brother would be committed to an asylum, though the possibility that he might made us laugh a lot. Above all, I think we wanted to cause embarrassment to our school, and to get our own back for so many beatings and restrictions of our liberty. The question likely to be asked far and wide, after our blow against tyranny, would be: 'What sort of school could be bad enough to have on its roll pupils prepared to write such stuff to an innocent girl?'

Knowing no girls ourselves, we had never thought of our classmate's sister as a real person who might be upset by our words. I doubt we would have sent our letter if we had. As for our own fate, like kamikaze pilots, we had brushed it aside. If there were to be victims, common sense should have told us that we would be among them. But joyfully anticipating the outcry we would shortly be causing, and confident that our forgery was perfect, we did not bother to plan our response, should the girl's brother deny authorship and be believed.

John Scott, my co-conspirator, found me in the tuck-box room shortly after lunch on the day following our letter's dispatch. He told me that the brother had just been sent for by the headmaster. When he remained absent for the whole of the first afternoon period, we were not surprised. He was back for the start of the next, and was not looking as upset as we had expected. I asked him in a stage whisper what the headmaster had wanted, and was told to mind my own business.

Unknown to us, the headmaster had already drawn up a list of those boys he thought were capable of writing such a letter. John and I were on it, as were two other boys, who in the eyes of Mr Ferrier, our headmaster, possessed the necessary skill and nerve. We were interviewed separately, then two at a time, then all together. We guilty ones gave away nothing. As fans of *The Wooden Horse* and *The White Rabbit* ('Vee vill keel you Preetish officer!'), we were not easily intimidated. Besides, our testicles were not about to be beaten black and blue with a rubber truncheon, nor would we be half-drowned in a bucket.

But when, two days later, we were summoned to the sixth form and the hoary old blackmailing formula was dusted down, the facts of our situation became clear to us at last. Three boys suspected we had done it, and one actually knew we had, since he had given John the address of the sister's school. Furthermore, there were six Sundays left in the term and the pressure on us to confess would get worse by the week. Eventually, we would be betrayed. So why wait? John and I agonized over what to do, while sitting in the grass beside the Hastings road. As passing cars whipped dust into our faces, we realized that our offence might be too serious for us to be forgiven, even after a beating. Expulsion might be inevitable if we confessed. But if we didn't confess, and were then forced to do so by betrayal, expulsion would be more likely than if we had volunteered our guilt at the outset.

There was another consideration: even if we escaped expulsion, the report, which the headmaster would send to our future public schools was certain to be damning. This could ruin our lives, we were sure. Why would our parents have sent us away, denying themselves our company, unless our time here had been essential to get us into a good school? Yet we had thrown away our character training: the cold showers, the runs, the beatings. No 'great school' could be expected to take us now – only some minor place that was short of pupils, and would never qualify us for an important job when we grew up. A term ago, a boy in our class had had to leave because his father had lost his money. I had been jealous of this boy for going home in term-time, but I had also pitied him. He had gone away weeping over his lost opportunities, and who could tell what his future held?

I thought of my mother's unhappiness at Charing Cross Station when I returned to school each term, and I felt sick with guilt. If her sacrifices had been for nothing, what would she say to me? John was also close to tears.

'My dad's a research chemist and earns peanuts.'

'So does mine.'

I suspected that in my position, my father would make a martyr of himself and take the whole blame. We'd recently read *A Tale of Two Cities* in class and I hadn't cared for the culminating act of self-sacrifice. Not that I wouldn't have granted John any reasonable favour. Recently, I'd been to his house in Sevenoaks and met his parents. His mother suffered from asthma, as did I. It had been a bond. Before I left, she told me about some pills that helped her breathe more easily and wrote down their name for me.

'They won't chuck you out, John,' I shouted above the roar of a lorry. 'You're the school's best batsman.'

We confessed on Saturday so that the school wouldn't be kept in detention the following afternoon. Although the waiting had been hard, we had delayed till evening, since, if beaten (and we expected six or more), it was best to be able to get to bed quickly, rather than endure a whole day sitting on hard seats. Our interview with the headmaster was not at all as we had imagined. Mr Ferrier was taken by surprise by our confession, and seemed at a loss for words. In the end, John asked him whether he was going to beat us.

He replied glumly: 'That won't answer, I'm afraid. I'll tell you what I've decided, after I've seen your parents next week.'

'Do you have to see them?' I whispered.

'I do.'

He then told us what an 'ungentlemanly' and 'dirty' thing we had done, dwelling on how shocked the girl had been. 'You two boys have disgraced your school.'

Perhaps considering this was an unsuitable mission for an ex-conscientious objector, my mother came on her own to see Mr Ferrier. By the time I got to hear her account of the interview, term had ended. I hadn't even been aware of the precise day on which she came, and she had left without seeing me, having kept her taxi waiting. My mother was barely five feet tall, and, on the eve of battle, was in her early fifties. Though she was fatter than was sensible for someone small, she could, when the occasion demanded, rise above her physical stature and give a commanding performance.

I only found out what had happened when the holidays came. My mother said brusquely that she wouldn't tell me everything. I'd done something 'perfectly idiotic' and owed her an apology. I apologized at once, and then sat beside her.

'Listen with Mother,' I muttered, failing to amuse her.

My mother tossed her head dramatically. 'Of course, I told him at once I wouldn't believe you'd done anything terrible unless he showed me the letter.'

'Golly! He wouldn't have liked that.'

'He blushed like a beetroot and said it wasn't the kind of letter he could show a lady. So I said I'd made a wasted journey and got up to go. He told me it was a bad enough letter to expel you for, and said I should trust him "on his word as a gentleman". I said several gentlemen *I* knew had told me that boys were only expelled these days for stealing

81

and bu . . . I can't tell you the word. It's something that lands men in prison.'

'What happened then?'

'Not much. He kept glancing round the room because he couldn't look me in the eye. Eventually, I asked what your godmother would think of him if he expelled boys for jokes that went wrong, and then produced no evidence. Then he admitted he hadn't made a final decision. So I knew I'd hit the mark. Cathie helped him start the place, you know.'

Although I was touched by my mother's defence and felt quite choky, I knew I owed her some honesty: 'It was quite a nasty letter, mummy.'

She looked at me sharply. 'You don't say.'

And that was all. She never spoke of it again and my father never referred to it at all. I'm sure, if she had confided in him, he would have deplored her bringing in my godmother, although that was probably what had saved me from expulsion. I had just been given a lesson in the importance of having useful connections, but I hadn't noticed.

Our punishment was announced a week after our confession. We were to be kept in detention every Sunday till term ended, and we would have no more visits from our parents. In addition, we were not to be made officers (prefects) next term, as our seniority in the school would otherwise have entitled us. Yet this would be no disaster. Since the precise nature of our offence was never mentioned by the authorities, it acquired an aura of mystery. Our kudos was destined to grow.

# EIGHT

For me, the 'letter incident' seemed to confirm my mother's role as my infallible protector. When I came home for the holidays, absence had definitely made my heart grow fonder; and I forgot how easy it would have been for her to have sent me to a London school in the first place. My love for her at this time was tinged with sympathy. I knew she had been disappointed with my father for years, and I admired her for not letting this make her disappointed with life.

For as long as I could remember, she had tried to make the best of the present, by getting to know new people, while keeping faith with old friends, such as her elderly accompanist, the marvellously named Daisy Bucktrout, who had played at her Wigmore Hall recitals, and Gertrude ('Toto') Norman, an actress, who had been in Sir Henry Irving's company for many years. Like my father, Toto was a believer in reincarnation, and hoped that she and her deceased American girlfriend – an opera singer in this life – would be reunited in the next.

My mother's circle of friends was neither fashionable nor aristocratic – though an Estonian baroness gave it the faint air of a court in exile. Often, things were not as they seemed. A close friend was the ballerina, Anna Ivanova, whose Russian name, and job, directing the Portuguese National Ballet, concealed the fact that she was really Nancy Handley from the north of England. Both my parents enjoyed the company of artists of all sorts. A painter, who often dined with them was Kyffin Williams (then the art master at Highgate School; now Sir Kyffin) whose powerful and sombre Welsh landscapes contrasted with his light-hearted and witty conversation. Other painter friends were Kathleen Browne (a frequent exhibitor at the Leicester Galleries) and her Polish husband, Marian Kratochwil, whose paper scissor-cuts delighted me as a child and whose paintings still do.

Eccentricity appealed to my mother, in all its forms, except the religious. A millionaire neighbour, Bartlett Judd, who dined with her once a month, took carefulness with money into realms where even my father feared to tread. He owned several properties in Kensington, and having painted his own house black during the war to hide it from the Luftwaffe, went on doing so in peacetime, on finding that the stucco required fewer repaintings than when painted white. He also covered much of his garden with green-stained boards, finding them cheaper to maintain than a lawn. His one extravagance was a pond overflowing with gigantic koi carp, earmarked for London Zoo in his will.

Someone my mother particularly enjoyed seeing was her cousin, Mona, widow of A. G. Macdonnell, author of the best-selling *England Their England* and the much anthologized short story 'The Cricket Match'. One evening in 1959, when Mona was dining with us, she was called to the telephone in the corridor to be told that her sister, Cathleen Queensberry, had just committed suicide. Rather than spoil my mother's party by telling us what had really happened, Mona said she had to leave because the elderly woman staying with her had locked herself out in the street. Mona had come through many tragedies – a humiliating divorce; her much loved second husband dying on-board ship returning from India; her son killed in the war; the love of her life marrying another woman just before she herself became free – all of which she endured without losing faith in her future. Mona's longstanding lover – an air ace in the First World War – came to see us almost as often as she. Despite his huge hands, he was expert at *petit point* embroidery. Another of my mother's favourites was a childhood friend, who had never fully recovered from being forced into the army by his father. This was Harry Chase, the old Marlburian whose name I had recklessly appropriated. His breakdowns persisted, as did my mother's sympathy.

My father was present at these dinners, though often drifting on thoughts of his own. When the admiral's candlesticks were gleaming on the table, and all the places set for dinner, my mother's cooking, and her obvious pleasure in entertaining, ensured that her parties lived on in the minds of her guests long after her candles had been snuffed out.

My mother's hospitality extended to her tenants, whom she cooked for when they were ill, and listened to in any personal crisis. Even those who returned to homes abroad kept in touch and visited whenever in England: a Dutch engineer, an American historian, a female Canadian chemist, who became a priest.

All her life my mother was a considerate employer. In later years, she kept on her aged 'daily', Mrs Statham, into her eighties – 'the old stick needs the money' – giving her tasks that could be done sitting down, such as cleaning silver and ironing, while employing a succession of 'resting' actors, from a Knightsbridge agency called 'Your Servant', for the heavier work. She often gave Mrs Statham money for a taxi home. When I told my mother I'd seen her taking the bus instead, she said: 'I don't mind if she'd rather save it.' Mrs Statham suffered from osteoporosis and was bent double by the time my mother suggested a reduction in her hours. At her own request she came for two afternoons a week, and continued coming until a few days before she died.

After I left home, the actors became an alternative source of maternal interest to my mother. Her favourite, Tom, was a gentle young man in his early twenties with dark curly hair, whom she reclaimed as her cleaner at the end of whatever acting job briefly removed him. My mother went to see him in pantomime and in various walk-on parts, and was delighted for him when he started making decent money in cabaret, in Beirut. When the civil war started, he returned to her and stayed on.

While I was at Westminster School – absurdly as an expensive weekly boarder, rather than a day boy – the electricity board, for which my father still worked, moved its metropolitan headquarters to the South Coast, and he was transferred to its regional headquarters in Surrey on a reduced salary. At this time, my sister, who had just left Cambridge, got married to the eldest son of the chairman of Mowlem's, the contractor. Despite my father's ongoing efforts to economize, Thomasina was treated to a Knightsbridge reception of some splendour, paid for out of our mother's dwindling 'free' capital. The bride's family always paid, and my mother would quite literally rather have died than break with tradition. Wearing a new hat, her best diamond brooch, and an outfit designed for the occasion, she appeared to relish 'doing things properly'. A few months later, she took in a third lodger, and I was moved out of my bedroom into a slit of a room – the smallest in the house – where I would stay for several years.

My parents thought their expenditure on my education was money well-spent, which it was from an academic perspective. Pastoral care was less impressive. A member of my house used chloroform to render boys unconscious so he could photograph them in the nude and sell his pictures in Soho. Meanwhile the headmaster of the day, John Carleton, made a habit of fondling boys when they came to him for their pre-confirmation chat. He was reputed to say: 'I always think joining the Christian Church is like joining a damned good club.' When my turn came, I found that he really *did* say this. I also found that by bracing my hands on my knees and leaning forward, I could stop him pushing me back on the sofa.

At the end of a silent trial of strength, he said to me, as if nothing had happened: 'At the ceremony, Tim, don't wear shoes with holes in their soles or the whole congregation will see them when you kneel at the sanctuary steps; and don't wear hair oil. It's common, and His Grace hates getting the stuff on his hands.'

School was my world, and I can only remember a single occasion on which my parents intruded – this was when my father decided he wanted to watch the school's football team play Charterhouse. He had seen, in *The Times,* an article about the centenary of this fixture.

'Parents never watch matches,' I explained, 'and boys only watch because they're told to. Sport isn't highly regarded at Westminster.'

'Why is that?' My father looked confused.

'Because boys who like games are usually dull.'

'I loved football as a boy.'

'I'm really sorry, daddy. I'm sure some of the first team are nice. But you really mustn't come. It's too difficult to explain, and you wouldn't understand if I tried.'

On the day of the match, I'd almost forgotten our conversation – in fact, I'd become quite involved with the football. But in the second half, the game became scrappy and my attention wandered. There was a children's hospital in Vincent Square, beside our playing field, and I spotted several sick boys gazing down at the game. To the left of the hospital, a man was standing on the steps of an ordinary house. I thought he was my father's double, but only for a moment.

A better boy than I was would have brought his father in through the gates at once – even *I* had to struggle hard not to do the decent thing. But somehow I managed to avoid looking in his direction until the game was over. Even now, I sometimes wish I had risked the ridicule of my peers.

# NINE

On the day I went to tell my father that his only brother had died, I found him resting on a small sofa in the sitting room, sipping a cup of milky coffee. It was a bright spring day and he was enjoying the warmth of the sun on his legs. My father started to cut up an apple with a small knife, offering me slices from time to time. He had loved fruit ever since I could remember. It was five years now since he had been diagnosed as having Parkinson's disease and, though his face had become less expressive and his movements clumsier, the L-dopa tablets had slowed his deterioration. As I looked at him, in neatly pressed flannels, sitting beneath a painting by Reynolds of an old soldier holding a massive key, I did not realize that I was gazing on my parent's world on the eve of its dissolution.

My father was sure to be devastated by the news of his brother's death, and I dreaded telling him. They had corresponded once a week for twenty-five years. Because Ted reminded him of their happy childhood, my father had remained devoted to him even after he'd moved from America to South Africa and had started writing articles favourable to apartheid, which my father detested. Unaware at first that his brother was investing his money in Johannesburg, not even the Sharpeville massacre, and the subsequent stock market collapse, quite destroyed my father's faith in his brother, though it had cost him half his capital. Even a passing reference to Ted would launch my mother into a diatribe on his supposed miserliness, egotism and incompetence.

After I told my father about his brother, he wept as if choking, the sound seeming very loud after the silence.

I must have first seen Ted when I was two years old, before he left England to work for the World Bank in Washington, but of course I have no memory of that time. In January 1963, with nine months to fill before I was due at Oxford, I decided to travel through Africa. This wasn't because I was eager to see my uncle, but because going to Africa seemed more adventurous than going to most other places. However, I knew it would be useful to have a relation in South Africa when I ended my journeying there and looked around for a job to pay for my airfare home.

Although few young people travelled outside Europe then, my parents raised no objection to my going. My mother may have imagined me driven by the same adventurous spirit that had fired her seafaring ancestors. Shortly before I left, she rummaged in her tin-lined chest and produced two Boer flags captured by her father. She thought a South African museum might like to have them.

I travelled overland from Cairo to Johannesburg, at first by Nile steamer, and thereafter by road and rail, and, briefly, between Khartoum and Entebbe by air. I arrived in South Africa four months after leaving home, expecting to stay with my uncle at first. But when I phoned him from the bus station, he said his flat was too small for us both, and he had booked me into the YMCA. (I never did get to see where he lived.) I met him in the dining room of the 'Y' an hour later.

With his paunch, his horn-rimmed spectacles, his bustling manner and staccato speech, all he seemed to have in common with my father was a liking for crumpled lightweight suits.

My uncle thumped his briefcase on the table, and after sifting through its contents, which included the remains of his picnic lunch, he found a piece of paper on which he had written the name of a school where the headmaster had 'virtually promised' him he would give me a job, and that of an advertising agency 'where they're positively crying out for creative young people like you'. The following day, I found that neither had any intention of employing me. My room-mate at the 'Y' was sympathetic. He had once worked for the British and Foreign Bible Society. Perhaps they might have something for me.

As it happened, they did. Several days later I found myself stocktaking in their Johannesburg office, trying to account for thousands of copies of the Bible, and an even greater number of pamphlets containing every part of the holy book, some no larger than Ezekiel, and all translated into a dozen southern African 'native' languages. Soon, I was sent out in a van to sell Bibles, and their parts, in local townships at a price which per page made lavatory paper seem expensive. I and two colleagues were chosen to judge an African choirs' contest – my only credentials being that I had sung in Westminster Abbey. Owing to a lapse in concentration, I allowed the representative of a losing choir to snatch from the table the envelope containing the winner's cash prize. In the near riot that followed, we were lucky to escape with our lives.

One evening, my Uncle Ted arrived at the 'Y' looking more pleased with himself than usual. He flopped down on my bed without asking and mopped the sweat from his bald head with a handkerchief.

'I've had a brilliant idea. You must join the University of the Witwatersrand.'

'But I've got a job,' I reminded him.

'Don't be a fool. You needn't attend any classes.'

'Then what's the point?'

'The point is that you won't have to pay rent or – and here's the beauty of it – you won't have to shell out for food either, till the end of term.' I was about to ask him what was so great about paying at the end of term, when the answer came to me. By then I would have earned enough to be able to pay the rent myself, and he would not have to lend me anything.

Ted was tugging anxiously at his grey toothbrush moustache. 'I asked your daddy to tell you to bring your English exam certificates. You do have them with you?'

'Yes.'

He beamed. 'Then you'll have no trouble enrolling.'

I didn't. My only problem was that all the arts and humanities residences were full, so I had to live in Cottesloe Mining Engineering Residence – a collection of nissen huts in a distant suburb. I felt very young and ill-at-ease, among these twenty-something student engineers. The rules of the place obliged me, as a fresher, to wear a large yellow bow-tie, and to greet the members of the house committee by name if I met them in a corridor. When the head of this student committee graduated, he underwent a bizarre rite of passage, in which he was stained black all down one side of his body, including half of his shaved head and half his genitals. Because I was seen as an effete oddity in this Afrikaner residence, some third-year students decided to shave off my hair as a side-show to the main event. I only escaped because two new friends, who were in the university's wrestling team, happened to arrive as I was being held down. In gratitude, I gave Hans and Don my grandfather's battle trophies.

Most days my uncle was busy with meetings at the Stock Exchange, or in his office in Commissioner Street. When we next met, he seemed relieved that I was off his hands. I did not tell him about the occasion on which my room was sandbagged and filled with water to a depth of four feet, nor that my windows had been taken out, used as barbecue trays, and never returned.

By the end of term I had left the biblical world, and was working as a radio actor in a South African Broadcasting Corporation children's drama, *The Prince, the Princess and the Cat,* as the eponymous prince. Every evening I was a wine steward in a nightclub. These jobs made it hard for me to attend functions at Cottesloe, though I acted in several sketches in a variety show during Rag Week. Ted amazed me by coming to this event and praising my performance. The following day, I was due to leave for Durban and a long weekend with people I had met while wine stewarding. My uncle spent the night in my bed, obliging me to sleep on the floor, so he could be on hand at first light to guide me to the best spot for hitchhiking to the coast. Otherwise, I might have wasted my money on a bus fare.

One day, when the time was approaching for me to leave South Africa, Ted summoned me to his office.

'What do you think?' he asked, indicating a couple of rolls of sludge-coloured cloth, balanced across his desk.

'What are they for?'

'Suits.' He held one up and examined it in the light. 'I haven't seen much of you, so I thought I'd give you something.'

'*Give* me something?' I was stupefied.

'Don't worry. My Indian tailor will make you a couple of suits for next to nothing. I give him investment tips.' My uncle handed me a scrap of paper. 'Here's his address. He'll need to take your measurements.'

The suits fitted me surprisingly well when they arrived in London three months later, but the material was worse than I remembered, so I rarely wore them. In the twenty years that followed, I wrote to Ted occasionally (always to a Post Office box rather than to an address). I never telephoned because he would have deplored the expense. For the same reason, he never sent Christmas or birthday presents to any of us. I never forgot him, but to be honest, he was rarely in my thoughts during the decades following our encounter in 1963.

A few days after breaking the news of his death to my father, I learned that the manner of his passing had been typical of his eccentric existence. In 1982, the year of his death, he was living on the veldt, ten miles from Johannesburg in North Riding, Randburg. Apparently, he still preferred, at the age of eighty, to hitchhike to the Stock Exchange each day rather than own a car. When he woke up one cold May morning to find his bronchitis worse than usual, he decided to get to Edenvale Hospital by hitching a lift. On arrival he lost no time booking himself in as a non-paying patient. Though diagnosed with double-pneumonia, he went on scribbling notes for the next issue of his monthly investment newsletter, *Rand Investment*. His last request, before the sudden heart attack that killed him, was to be taken to the nearest telephone so he could speak to Monty Silverman, his stockbroker.

When I flew out to organize my uncle's funeral, I was curious to see where he had lived. Armed with a map provided by Mr Silverman, I drove out of town for half-an-hour, then left the highway and bounced along a dirt track for another mile or two through scrubland, before coming upon a tin-roofed range of half-converted farm buildings. None appeared to have been completed by their builders, even for their original agricultural purpose. Most were let to young people on low incomes, several of whom were lying low to dodge their military service. Bizarrely, my uncle's personal living quarters had once been a pigsty, and their conversion to human use had been so poorly done that the doors and windows were all drunkenly askew.

Next to my uncle's desk stood a wheelbarrow containing dried cement, and beside it plasterboard sheets were piled high. The concrete floor was untiled, the walls unpainted, and, most surprising of all, there was no glass in any of the windows and no sign of a heater. It was winter now, and very cold at night. Ted's miserliness had literally been the death of him. What had he used to eat, I wondered, looking at the chaos of broken cane chairs and builders' rubbish in the kitchen corner. The cooker was buried under a mound of dusty papers and, nearby, a brown loaf, bearing the teeth marks of rats, and a rotting avocado, suggested that my uncle's diet had been simple. Tattered clothing spilled from a tin trunk. There was no bed, just a mattress and bedding on the floor behind a partition.

I asked one of his tenants whether my uncle had ever seemed depressed by his surroundings. The young woman grinned at me.

'He never noticed them.'

Every surface, whether chair, table, stove, decrepit cupboard, or carpenter's planks, was covered in papers. Papers also filled dozens of carrier bags. The man who had worked for the World Bank, the Control Commission in Berlin, and then for Price Waterhouse and Deloitte Plender, had long been a stranger to any kind of filing. In the chaos, I found a photograph of my uncle in a major's uniform during the war, looking spick and span in his Sam Browne belt. In another picture, he was with his horse in the South African countryside.

At Ted's bank, the day before, I had been amazed to hear that two decades earlier – the very time of my earlier visit – he had been worth several million rands. I was advised to throw away nothing, neither old demands for rates, nor utility bills, which might help me trace development properties and other investments he had never mentioned to anyone. His strangest visible investment was a consignment of about two hundred replacement windows for railway carriages, now lying in a vast pyramid to the side of the path. The most evocative find in the entire place consisted of several mouldering rolls of cloth, evidently part of a job lot, and identical to those he had given me for my suits in 1963.

His electricity supply had been cut off, but the lack of artificial light and the eerie silence did not stop me working by torchlight long after the sun had gone down over the veldt. By one in the morning, I had found a few rate demands for some seaside plots outside Durban. I had also turned up some personal documents. The few letters from women were dated years ago; and several photographs, which I assumed were of a former girlfriend, were yellowing with age. At some stage he had chosen to lead this solitary and obsessive life. The funniest letter I found was the carbon of an enraged rant, sent to the head of the South African Broadcasting Corporation, castigating him for allowing the broadcast of a Test Match between England and Australia (South Africa was excluded from international cricket at the time) to delay the evening stock market report.

Ted would turn out to be significantly poorer than his bank manger had led me to expect. However, the Argentine junta's unexpected attack on the Falklands spiked up the gold price dramatically, taking the rand with it. In the end, thanks initially to General Galtieri, and then to Mrs Thatcher, my uncle's estate would be worth rather more than had seemed likely a few weeks earlier.

One of my uncle's tenants must have told the Johannesburg *Sunday Times* that 'old uncle Edward' would be a good subject for an article. Anyway a journalist from that paper unearthed most of Ted's acquaintances, and ran me to ground at my hotel. Under the banner headline of THE TYCOON IN A PIGSTY, and the subheading, LIVED WITH RATS BUT HIS LOYALTY WAS TO GOLD, the story of this latter-day Silas Marner was told with would-you-believe-it glee over six columns of an inside page.

He handled millions of rands of clients' money from many countries . . . but lived in unbelievable squalor and meanness . . . But all accepted him. His brilliant mind and sense of humour seemed to compensate for his strange ways . . .

On my return to London, I was surprised to find a letter from the South African Minister of Finance awaiting me. Mr

Horwood began by apologising for not writing sooner with his condolences:

> But I have been heavily involved in preparing our Budget, and am now in the throes of the Budget debate . . . Your uncle was a remarkable person – eccentric, perhaps, but extremely able and discerning, and possessed of a lively, concise style of writing. As a critic, informed and incisive, he was in a class almost of his own, in my experience. I miss his illuminating and frank correspondence, and am honoured to think he thought something of me. He was one of the most consistent economists I ever met, and just as sound.

# TEN

One evening, a few weeks after my return from South Africa, my mother telephoned. She was upset and emotional. Apparently, my father was behaving oddly and could not get into bed. His collapse was the more distressing since, for almost five years, the drugs prescribed by the hospital had enabled him to walk better and, when out alone, very rarely 'to get stuck', as my mother still described the occasional involuntary freeze-up.

'What do you mean by "behaving oddly"?'

'He makes no sense at all.'

'Maybe he's given himself a double dose of his drugs. You know what his memory's like.'

By the time I reached Earl's Court, my mother had somehow got my father into bed. He sat up as I entered his bedroom, looking flushed and excited. I hadn't been in his room for years, but it came as no surprise that the walls had not been painted for decades. His bed apart, the only piece of furniture was a beautiful Georgian desk. Above his head hung an abstract painting of the crucifixion – by Victor Galliano, another artist friend – in which Christ and the two thieves were symbolized as gigantic blue and orange fishes, standing on their tails.

My father held out his hands to me. 'Bravo, Tim! Any later and I'd have left for the City. Some men are coming for me on a motorbike.'

'Dear God!' muttered my mother, from the doorway.

'Who are these men?' I asked.

He was about to answer, when sudden bewilderment overtook him. 'It was on the tip of my tongue.'

'What was?' demanded my mother.

'What was what?' His expression was concerned but not seriously worried as his train of thought thundered off the rails.

We went to the sitting room and my mother sank down onto a sofa.

'Be an angel, and get us some whisky.' I went down to the dining room, poured us a glass each and returned with a small jug of water and our drinks. My mother poured water into hers and took a gulp. 'I've rung his doctor, who's arranging for him to go into St Mary Abbotts tomorrow. I'm not at all hopeful.'

Her pessimism upset me. Ever since my chat with my father on the Heath, I'd felt fairly confident that if his rational powers survived, so too would his religious faith, and with it his ability to cope.

Soon after my father's illness had been diagnosed, I'd bought a book called *Parkinson's Disease: The Facts* by two neurologists. They had shed no light on the disease's origins, nor on what long exposure to L-dopa might do to the brain; but they stated that during treatment, 'confusion, and vivid visual hallucinations', were sometimes 'provoked' by the drug and its derivatives. I told my mother this, and suggested that he would probably be fine again after a change in his dose.

'I think I'll end up as mad as him, if he stays the way he is.'

Although my mother's cleaner, Tom, was always liberal in his use of pine disinfectant, the smell of cats' urine and cooked fish coming up from the kitchen, immediately below us, was even stronger than usual. Since my father had become ill, the number of my mother's cats had increased to an outrageous seventeen. Nothing my sister or I had been able to say in recent months had persuaded her to moderate her obsessive cat collecting. We both hated to see her tossing aside her former fastidiousness as if it had never mattered.

One of my mother's tenants had just left (probably to escape the smell), so I was able to sleep in the empty room on the night before my father went into hospital. This top-floor bedroom had been mine briefly, before I left for Oxford, nineteen years earlier. It was a warm June night, and gazing out of the window at the moonlit bay tree in the garden and the privet hedge, everything looked deceptively as it had done in my childhood – except that everything about my parents' lives had altered, irretrievably. The only book in the room was a romance by Evelyn Anthony, left by the departing tenant along with some discarded safety razors and a broken plate. To stop myself thinking, I read a few pages before turning out the light. I didn't expect to fall asleep, but I did so almost at once.

My father seemed quite rational in the morning, and even said he was pleased his doctor had managed to get him a bed in the hospital at short notice. He searched his shelves for a book to take with him. Was I right to feel flattered that his choice was *Father and Son* by Edmund Gosse? He also took his Order of the Cross bible, *The Master*, which he had considered sacred enough to protect with a tartan wool cover. I went with him to St Mary Abbotts Hospital in the morning, and later my wife, Joyce, brought down our middle daughter, Lucy, then aged eight, to see him. She had amazed both Joyce and me – neither of us being musicians – by starting to play Mozart violin concertos a month or two earlier. She played for 'grandpa' now and tears filled his eyes.

He spoke quite sensibly to me at times during the morning, so I fetched my mother in the afternoon. To start with I was glad I had, but just when my confidence was growing, he turned to my mother and said in an earnest undertone:

'They run a furniture business in the basement, you know.'

I told him firmly that this was a hospital with no connection at all to the furniture trade. He sighed, as if vexed with himself for getting this wrong. But a moment later, he turned to me with a worried frown.

'You're quite sure about that, are you?' My mother hid her face in her hands.

Outside in the corridor, I tried to persuade her that occasional lapses into confusion weren't the end of the world. They were tinkering with his drugs, and couldn't be expected to get things right straightaway. She remained entirely unconvinced. Before we went home, my mother and I were seen by a courteous and softly spoken Pakistani neurologist, who explained that my father's drugs needed to be 're-balanced'.

'Will he stop talking nonsense when you've "balanced" him?' asked my mother.

'We should be able to help him.'

'What do you mean by "should be"?'

'Some patients with advanced Parkinson's have problems with dementia – not all, or even most – so I hope your husband isn't affected. We have to find out.'

I asked: 'Do you think the drugs could have damaged his brain?'

'More likely it's the way the illness is progressing in his case. Remember, he's been ill for years.'

We sat outside on a bench under some plane trees. It was a muggy summer's day and rain seemed imminent. My mother wept openly, the first time I had seen her cry since the trouble with Mrs Coley, when I was a child. I felt like doing the same.

'Maybe they'll manage to sort him out,' I faltered.

She brushed her tears away with the back of a hand. 'Come on, Tim, you're forty, not four.'

My mother stared down at the scuffed grass and the mess of cigarette ends at her feet, and said almost angrily: '*Any-thing* would be easier than this.'

Back home again, she rallied, though we both said very

little while drinking our tea. With no idea what might happen next, neither of us wished to explore our uncertainties.

I was back at St Mary Abbotts two days after my father's admission, hoping that alterations to his dosage might already have improved his mental functions. I found him in a chair by his bed, staring with a beatific smile at the roof of the building opposite. He heard my steps and turned.

'Just look at them!' My father pointed at the perfectly ordinary slate roof of the ward-block. 'Such happy children! What fun they're having on the beach. Even the fat boy on the donkey.' He chuckled indulgently.

He was wearing a shirt and jacket I had never seen before, as if they had changed his clothes along with his mind when he had been admitted. My father motioned me closer.

'It's quite a scandal,' he whispered, 'the nurses had a party in here last night. They had us out of bed for hours.'

'Doing what?'

'Dancing.'

'*Dancing?*'

'Oh, you know. Scottish reels and such like.'

'I don't think that's very likely.'

'One of them pinched my nose. Hurt like hell.' He reflected a moment. 'Quite funny though. They were using thermometers as cocktail sticks with pickled onions stuck on the ends.' He laughed at the memory.

I couldn't help laughing too, although I was scared. Would we ever have a normal conversation again? Perhaps a kind of death had taken place already. Certainly, I wouldn't be able to bring my mother to see him this afternoon. He jerked his head towards the people visiting his neighbour. His expression had changed to one of deep anxiety.

'You see those loaves of bread, Tim?' Could he really

mean the man and the woman sitting a few feet away?

'They're people,' I insisted.

Ignoring me, he murmured: 'Who will eat them? It's what I could never abide: waste of any kind.'

An uneasy grin hovered on the face of one of the loaves. I lowered my eyes, rapidly.

When I went to see my mother half-an-hour later, she asked me how he had been.

'Not so good today.'

Strangely, this euphemism stuck in her mind, and I would often hear her telling friends on the telephone: 'Joe's not so good today,' seeming to imply that on other days he had been better, and might be again.

On the following afternoon, I was told by the ward sister that my father had been unsettled for a second night and had been put on tranquillizers. He was seated in a different chair, with a bar fixed across it to stop him getting up, and his smiles had been replaced by an expression of over-whelming misery. What could they be doing to him? As I approached, he embarked on a rambling account of how a family in Kent was trying to take away his money. Their name was Robinson and, if I had any sense, I would watch out for them too.

'The name's English, but they speak with Scotch accents.'

My father was dribbling quite badly and he kept darting glances behind him, as though a Robinson might be creeping up on him.

By waiting outside his consultant's room for an hour, I managed to snatch a few words with Mr Khan and I begged him to take my father off tranquillizers. I admitted he had been confused yesterday but insisted he had not been unhappy in the horrible way he was now. Mr Khan agreed to stop the sedation and kept his word. It would be ten days, he told me, before he would know with confidence what level and combination of drugs would be best.

My father was still 'not so good' when he went home two weeks later, but he was capable of behaving normally for extended periods, and he did not hallucinate, except very occasionally in the evening. My mother was overjoyed to have him home.

My sister and I were glad for her, but while this uneasy, scarcely manageable phase lasted, she and I and Joyce began to look for places which might take in my father, or both my parents. My mother sometimes spoke, without much conviction, of finding 'a little flat', as if knowing that her only realistic options were to go with my father to an institution, or stay on in the house alone.

One evening, several weeks later, my mother rang and could hardly get her words out. I imagined my father had fallen down the stairs or had a seizure.

'It's not *him*,' she cried out with exasperation. 'We've been burgled. All my darling mother's treasures gone!'

I rang the police and then drove to Earl's Court. My mother was flustered and angry as she ushered me downstairs to the scene of the crime. She had forgotten to put in her teeth and was wearing a very old silk dressing gown. Had she been awake, she would definitely have confronted the thief with the whalebone cosh she kept by her bed. This antique weapon had been in her hand fifteen years earlier when she'd had the good luck and agility to frighten off a would-be robber. Fortunately for her, she'd been having a nap when this recent intruder had climbed through a basement window.

Before the police arrived, I spotted the imprint of a trainer's sole on the windowsill – how many millions with that pattern,

I wondered, were in existence? Around the room, cats sat staring down at me from the tops of the dishwasher and the refrigerator, and from boxes balanced on higher shelves.

'A pity *they* didn't attack the thief,' I muttered, trying not to breathe through my nose and smell their trays. As always, my mother seemed oblivious to the state of the room.

There was usually a pile of plastic bags, most of them marked 'MacFisheries', on the kitchen window seat, but now this seat was disconcertingly bare. I later deduced that the thief had hurried back to the kitchen for bags, having first entered the adjoining dining room and seen my mother's display cabinet with its Cantonese ivory chess set, Japanese netsukes, and museum-quality porcelain and glass. Back in the dining room, he also found the Pasley silver, and my Hastings grandmother's delicate Irish serving dishes and sauce boats. Even my father's few silver-handled knives found their way into a MacFisheries bag.

My mother took me into the dining room where the doors of the cabinet were still open, as were the sideboard drawers where the silver had been kept. She sat with her head bowed before banging the table.

'I'd have killed the brute if I'd got my hands on him.'

'Lucky, you didn't.'

'I'd have enjoyed it.'

Several years earlier, security bolts had been fitted to the kitchen windows, enabling them to be locked in an open position – the gap at the bottom being just large enough for cats to crawl in and out. Unfortunately, my mother was forever unscrewing these bolts and forgetting she had done so. Forgetfulness seemed responsible for today's events. At least this burglary had come after my mother had lost the will to entertain – not that this violated room did not strike me as a deeply melancholy place.

The detective constable, who came from Chelsea police station, asked my mother and me to compile a list of what had been taken. We did our best, assisted by an inventory of insured property and the schedule of heirlooms. I found I could only recall about half the items taken from the cabinet. Though pessimistic about their chances, the police went through the motions, dusting surfaces for fingerprints and asking a few questions. I gave them a bookplate of the Pasley arms, and since most of the silver was crested, this made them a little more hopeful. I myself visited about half-a-dozen West End shops specializing in oriental ivory, but saw no chess set matching ours exactly. Not a single item would ever be recovered, silver, ivory or porcelain.

The aspect of the burglary that grieved my mother most was that she had lost her mother's most valuable possessions which, unlike the heirlooms, might otherwise have come to my sister and me. One of my earliest memories dates from the year following my grandfather's death, when my mother had still not come to terms with the fact that her own father – who had lived with her and been nursed by her in his last illness – had effectively cut her and her children out of his will, in favour of his nephew, the new baronet. This nephew's solicitor had been about to arrive in order to make an inventory of the heirlooms (which my mother was entitled to 'enjoy' during her lifetime), when she burst out to my father: 'It's monstrous we have to put up with Rodney's lawyer poking about the place.' Her remark lodged in my memory, and when a waste-pipe became blocked several months later, and a man thrust some sort of flexible rod down it, the word association between rod and Rodney led me to assume that it must be *him* 'poking about' in our lavatory.

My mother was not angry with Rodney for what her father had done – he was clearly not to blame for that – but she was incandescent when she found that some of her mother's money, along with bomb-damage compensation paid by the government for her own blitzed furniture, had become mixed up with her father's estate. Although Rodney refused to release either sum – his son, Malcolm, would one day willingly restore both, to my sister and me. But long before that, my mother decided, for no reason she ever shared with me, to end her years of hostility towards her cousin.

I must have been over seventeen when this happened, because on the appointed day I drove the claret-coloured Wolseley, which my father had unexpectedly purchased in his mid-sixties with cash from a forgotten life-policy. My mother's olive branch took the form of handing over, in her lifetime, the largest Pasley heirloom. This enormous gold tureen stood on a wide base with tritons at its corners and with an elaborate lid, crowned by the figure of Father Neptune. It had been made for the first baronet shortly after the Battle of the Glorious First of June, with money raised by subscription at Lloyd's Coffee House. 'A Tribute of Respect from his Country' was engraved on the tureen. The 'tribute' was duly placed in the back of the Wolseley, and we drove away to lunch with Rodney in his stockbroker Tudor house in semi-rural Surrey.

I had looked forward to our visit because 'Johnny', Rodney's wife, was said to be able to detect water and buried metal with a dowsing rod. Another skill was using a pendulum to pinpoint the precise spot in people's bodies where they were experiencing pain or growing a tumour. My father was thrilled to see her pendulum in action, successfully detecting which of my mother's hips had been replaced – a task I would have thought more impressive if human beings had as many hips as vertebrae. My father told me that Johnny's powers arose from her 'inner harmony' which put her in touch with the 'outer harmony' of the universe. Johnny rarely came to London, but Rodney was a regular visitor. In future, he would dine with my mother whenever researching in the London Library, and would seem to grow quite fond of her in the years that remained to him.

During the summer of 1982, the cat situation worsened to the point where even my mother had to acknowledge that she was no longer able to take care of them without my father's help. She and Tom were struggling to deal hygienically with their numerous food dishes and trays, but the worsening stink proclaimed their failure. My father – though only marginally less lucid than after his return from hospital – had nevertheless become weaker in recent months. He suffered several spectacular falls, one of them down a whole flight of stairs. Incredibly, he broke no bones.

One day, I was shocked to see that he could only reach his bedroom by crawling upstairs on his hands and knees. He was still attempting to help my mother with the cats, but the sight of him trying to clean a tray, with urine dripping onto his shoes, was too upsetting to be borne. His fondness for these scrawny animals, and his awareness that they would have to go, made his determination not to let down my mother especially harrowing.

Whenever I tried to talk to my mother about the situation, she became angry. 'I'm not ready to kill them yet,' she would snap, as if I'd suggested phoning the vet that very moment. My sister and I took our mother to see several cat sanctuaries outside London. 'Horrible places,' she declared loudly, while still on the premises.

Every time I went to the house, I would be bitten by fleas, and the smell would seem to stick to me. I had started to loathe my mother's obstinacy. By now she had stopped shopping and was feeding my father from tins bought long ago.

She dragged out the cat crisis by enlisting the help of an elderly Irish woman from Fulham, who operated a one-woman private cat-welfare service. Mrs Giddens came every day and, for a while, postponed the inevitable.

When I had almost given up hope of anything changing, my mother came to a decision. Her voice on the telephone sounded calm, but I wasn't fooled by the absence of emotion.

'I can't manage Joe myself, so he'll have to go to a place where they can.'

'What about you?' I asked. Could she really intend to abandon my father? 'Will you be staying where you are?'

There was a long, tense silence. At last she said: 'I'll go into a zoo with him.'

Apart from feeling relief, I was proud of her for choosing to stay with him and leave her home. The reference to a 'zoo' was no surprise to me. Some years ago, the large house at the end of my parents' garden had become an old people's home. While tending plants on her trellis, my mother had talked to an old lady who lived there and who fed pigeons on her windowsill. 'Don't let anyone put you in a zoo like this one,' the bird lover had warned my mother. After telling this anecdote, my mother assured me that she would never want to live with my sister or me. By letting her own father live under the same roof as my father, she admitted she had harmed her marriage. A home, she told me, was the only option.

The problem of the cats remained unresolved, but not for long. Rejecting further talk of animal sanctuaries, my mother summoned the vet and told him to put down three.

'I had James, Horse and Spinny killed this morning,' she informed me tersely, when I happened to ring her the same evening.

These were only the first to go. Other animals would soon be taken to the basement bathroom and injected while my mother held them. I came to dread her phone calls. I often puzzled over why she should have accumulated all these cats just when she was least able to cope with them. Perhaps it was due to a subconscious need to be diverted from my father's illness. After several weeks of lethal injections, only two cats were left alive. And now my mother's formidable will deserted her. These survivors she could not kill.

In August, Joyce succeeded in finding a residential home that answered my parents' requirements. It was called Woodstock and was run by an organization called the Hampstead Old People's Housing Trust. Incredibly, Joyce had approached the trust just when they had two vacancies – the available accommodation consisting of two adjoining bed-sitting rooms, and a sole-use bathroom, as well as a small kitchen that could be used if my parents should ever want a change from the meals provided in the dining room. Although this flatlet was in the basement of a large Victorian mansion, the rooms looked on to a spacious garden, itself on the edge of Primrose Hill. My sister and I pleaded with the three women who ran the trust to allow my mother to bring her last two cats with her. After a lengthy interview, they agreed.

And so the day came for my mother to leave her home of thirty years for the last time. My father was again in St Mary Abbotts for 're-balancing', so only my mother climbed into my sister's Peugeot. Tom, the cleaner, was in tears, and so were Joyce and I as we waved to the departing car. I wasn't thinking of the painful year we had all just been through, but of brighter days when my sister had still lived here, and when I'd returned from boarding school for the holidays, and when we had all belonged here, in the street I'd taken for granted.

Still in the front garden, Joyce and I waited for the new Pasley baronet, Sir Malcolm – Sir Rodney having died – to come and collect the Reynolds, Kneller and Beechey family portraits.

The house across the street, where T. S. Eliot's future bride had once lived, was now a brothel, its balcony surmounted by a gilded nude. Respectable looking businessmen were already arriving for their appointments, as my cousin's estate car drew up. After the emotional events of the morning, the need to make small talk to Malcolm – a likeable and mild-mannered Oxford don, as he strapped the largest portrait (my childhood pirate) onto his roof rack – added a note of absurdity to the proceedings which, until then, had been wholly sad. Would our ancestor survive his windswept journey to Malcolm's semi-detached house in north Oxford? Yes, we both reckoned he would. 'After all, he came through the Blitz,' I burbled, for the sake of saying something, 'and wasn't even touched when my parents' flat was hit. Lucky they were out at the time.'

Back in the familiar house, the empty squares of clean wallpaper, where the portraits had so recently been taken down, told me as eloquently as boarded-up windows would have done, that this was no longer anyone's home. I walked into the sitting room of the now catless house, where I had grown up. To my amazement, scores of fleas leapt up from the carpet to greet me.

# ELEVEN

To make my father's bureau lighter for the removals men, I had removed its contents – books, notebooks and papers – and had taken them home with me for safekeeping. This was how I first came to dip into his little meditation notebooks, and to read entries, such as: 'The purpose of my life is to *become* – to live in the consciousness of God's presence, always his Child . . .'

My greatest surprise was to read his account of how, in 1944, he had been on the verge of achieving 'Oneness with God', coming close enough 'to hear the divine voice reverberating through the planes of my consciousness'. Only fear of losing his identity had held him back. His friend, Dame Ethel Walker – whose symbol-filled paintings were then hanging in the entrance hall of the National Gallery – tried to reassure him in a letter: 'Though I lose my self entirely when I paint, the higher Being who raises me up does not annihilate me.'

At this time, my father had left the army, and was living alone in the Kensington flat – the family having moved to Oxford to escape the flying bombs. One night he returned home and slept for a few hours, before waking to find himself on the brink:

The Presence came impellingly and I could hardly resist. But I did – failed. It was all in my ears and throat. Then I slept and again awoke and resisted. Then I dreamt of my Airborne Div. pals in lovely hills . . . I shall not resist again.

But eleven days later, he *did* resist again:

It was something indescribable about the Divine Activity which made me fail. It was gem-like, magnetic and yet <u>too</u> lovely – mixing sweetness with intensity and power.

To his bewilderment and grief, days became weeks and 'the Presence' stayed away. Nothing saved my father from his sense of failure, but he found some consolation in the work of the Russian existentialist, Nicolas Berdyaev, and in Indian writings about *Karma* – the law of moral causation, whereby a man is only perfected after many lives. Yet the more I read, the clearer it became to me that my father still hoped to achieve the crown of mystical experience in this lifetime. So would he, at this late stage, experience 'One-ness' through the 'second chance' which illness had given him? If only.

When I returned my father's papers, he was still in hospital and my mother was impatient for him to arrive at Woodstock. As I re-stocked his desk, my mother sat on his bed. With his furniture finally in place, and the abstract painting of the crucifixion hanging above his bed, his new room was almost indistinguishable from his former bedroom, except for having much whiter walls.

My mother had been glancing at one of my father's Order of the Cross printed booklets, and now tossed it aside. 'Complete gobbledegook. Joe once told me these books were written in "the language of symbols".'

'Did he say why?'

'To get us to remember our past lives.' She sniffed derisively. 'Did Joe tell you that when Todd Ferrier had his visions, he was a low church minister in Macclesfield?'

'He should have been an Anglican vicar in Hampshire?'

'You knew very well what I meant.' Opening a notebook at random, she read aloud: 'The solution to every problem is already in being, and it is for us to find it. Where? In the Peace within ourselves, of course.' She closed the book abruptly. 'My God, if it was only that easy. How is Joe going to cope with his illness "from within himself"?'

'He's never complained or been angry about it.'

'*I'm* the one who's angry. Think of all the old horrors who go on forever without a day's illness and never did a kind turn to anyone. Yet your father never stopped doing good deeds.'

I didn't disagree. Over the years, he'd done his best to help numerous friends – whether they were moving house, changing job, or finding a new art gallery. These friends were from all walks of life and included people he had met in shops and in parks. A surprising number had turned out to share his interests.

Estella Canziani, he had met feeding pigeons near the Round Pond in Kensington Gardens. She lived in Palace Green, Kensington Palace Gardens, often called Millionaires' Row, in a house that had once been Queen Anne's laundry. The battered old black copper, in which the queen's sheets had been boiled, could still be seen in a gardener's shed when I used to visit. The house itself was a low rambling building, enclosed by an overgrown garden, and sandwiched between ambassadorial residences. Estella was in her late sixties when my father first introduced us. She owned a fine collection of Renaissance painted glass, and had herself been a successful water-colourist, writer and book illustrator. Her best known picture was the much reproduced *Piper of Dreams*.

As a child, I was fascinated by the birds in her aviary and in the house itself. In her garden, doves would flutter down out of the mulberry trees and perch on her pudding basin hat. Although she hated modern Kensington and rarely left her enclosed world, on the last occasion I saw her she told me she had recently seen a monk's ghost in the Earl's Court Road outside Rassells' garden nursery.

'I hurried after him to get a glimpse of his face, but there was nothing under his cowl.'

Far from finding this Bergmanesque vision creepy, my father nodded approvingly. 'You should keep your eyes open too,' he murmured in my direction.

He had been in the tube when he had met his future friend, Ronald Jerome, a teacher of religious studies at Emanuel School. Jerome wore a blatant black wig and lived in Wimbledon Park in a small terraced house, containing an impressive collection of historic clocks, later donated to the Victoria & Albert Museum. His ceilings had been strengthened to take the weight of two massive seventeenth-century chandeliers. He also collected Italian pictures and French furniture. His little house was so unusual that I took Joyce to meet him there. We were invited to stay for an early supper of spam and lettuce, surrounded by his treasures.

A keen supporter of his local church, Jerome took delinquent boys on expeditions. My father and I were once invited to help him shepherd a dozen such boys to hear Billy Graham at Wembley. As we sat with them in a minibus, I was haunted by Evelyn Waugh's aphorism about it being 'very hard for a man with a wig to keep order'. Luckily, our boys seemed oblivious to the fraudulence of Jerome's hair. In the stadium, they were mesmerized by the evangelist – so when he called out thrillingly: 'I appeal to each and every one of you who has found Jesus to come onto the pitch and join me there,' most of our charges hurried down to affirm their brand new faith. They had found God, but would we find *them* when the crowds surged along Wembley Way? My father said we would, and he turned out to be right.

Through Jerome, my father met Herbert Austin, a clock-maker. My father once told me that, if he had ever been able to start again, he would have loved to master a craft like Austin's, but doubted whether he had the manual skill. Every clock in my parents' house was overhauled by Austin, whom I often met at work there. By the early 1970s such men were rarities, which only increased my father's respect.

While still waiting for my father to leave hospital, my mother did her best to get used to eating in the large dining room with people whom she didn't know. She told me that the man who 'called himself a major' was no such thing, and that some of the old ladies snatched at the cream jug, and took all the 'baby tomatoes' from shared salads.

One day, she said she felt sorry for the lonely people who sat in the hall for hours at a time, watching the comings and goings.

'You'd better strangle me if *I* start doing that.'

Some of her attitudes were snobbish but she was not a snob. Her aristocratic aunts had dropped her after she married my father, and this had left her determined never to judge people purely on the basis of class. But she was very sensitive about being patronized; and when cheerful young people, wearing boaters and striped blazers came and sang 'Old Time Songs', she wasn't one of the nice old ladies who sang along with them. Matron enraged my mother by entering her room without knocking. I suggested that it might pay to be diplomatic rather than risk antagonizing such people, but I was told it was 'a great mistake to let anyone walk all over one, unless one meant to go on like that'.

In these early days at Woodstock, my mother didn't complain, but she didn't express any pleasure either. On an upper landing in my house, I was accommodating my mother's display cabinet, which still contained a few items the thief had left behind. On her first visit to my house since moving to Primrose Hill, she gazed through the glass doors of her cabinet as if unable to tear away her eyes.

'My God,' she said, turning to me at last. 'There really *is* life after death. I must tell your father.'

'How do you work that out?'

'When people are dead, their possessions end up in other people's houses. But here am I, very much alive and looking at them in your house now.'

'Now there's a cheering thought,' I murmured.

My mother seemed pleased to have got through to me. At any rate, she smiled. I knew better than to say: 'Things can't be as bad as all that, can they?' Remembering my time at boarding school, I did not have to imagine what it was like to be trapped among people I had not chosen to be with. There was something very disturbing about our changed positions. She was in an institution now, just as I had been years ago, and I could visit and take her out as I chose.

'I'm sure matron hates me,' my mother informed me on the phone. (I had a sense of *déjà vu*. Hadn't I said something very like that too?) 'She's furious I won't let anyone clean my room when I'm out.'

'What did she say precisely?'

'That I don't trust her staff. But that's not true. I just don't want my things to be moved about, unless I'm there.'

I feared that my mother's outspoken manner would lead to more misunderstandings. But with luck, my father's gentle way with people would disarm them before her directness started to ruffle any more feathers. So it was a relief when I finally heard from my father's consultant that he was ready to be discharged.

On a bright September morning, I drove my father along the Cromwell Road past the turning to his old home, past Gloucester Road, past the Natural History Museum and the V&A. He was wearing his Alfred Kemp bookie's jacket, and a pair of pinstripe trousers that I'd never seen before. Mysterious transformations of his wardrobe were commonplace while he was in hospital. He was looking around happily.

'Such glorious planes,' he remarked, glancing up at the plane trees along the road, rather than at the usual West London aeroplanes.

I thought of him cycling this very route several times a week only a couple of years ago on his way to Harrods to buy fish. What must he be feeling as the familiar landmarks rolled by, into his past? A look of intense inner concentration told me he was certainly feeling *something* as Brompton Oratory slipped by to the left.

As we came level with Harrods, he grasped my arm. 'We have to stop.'

'It's not a brilliant place.'

'Can't be helped. I've got to pee.'

I gazed out at expensively dressed passers-by, many of them women, and said: 'There are loos in Harrods.'

He looked at me as if I was mad. 'I can't wait.'

I stopped the car and twisted round to see if there was anything on the back seat or on the floor that he could pee into. My eye fell on my youngest daughter's school sandwich container. I ripped it open and tossed out an empty juice carton and a plastic spoon.

'There.'

Struggling with old-fashioned fly-buttons, he was too busy to thank me. 'Give me a hand, damn it.'

There, in the heart of fashionable Knightsbridge, I extricated my father's penis from his underpants and thrust it into my daughter's 'Snoopy' lunch box, while the modish world rolled by.

As we swept past Lord's Cricket Ground on our way to Primrose Hill, I told him how much my mother was looking forward to his arrival. He said nothing until we stopped in Elsworthy Road. Then, outside the large Edwardian house, he turned to me solemnly:

'Those fish tanks under the house, are they still there?'

'They never were.'

'I suppose I must accept what you say.' He looked so crestfallen that I wished I could tell him his senses had not deceived him.

'Please don't say a word about fish tanks to Norah.'

'I'll try.'

My mother was in the garden when we arrived, so I took him out at once, and was touched when she rose from her chair and kissed him on the cheek. How marvellous it would be if he could remain more or less normal for a year or so. I watched as he sat down at her table, amazed to see them still together.

In their first months at Woodstock, my parents would often chat while my mother worked on an enormous patchwork quilt. In the evenings they watched television or listened to music. Once an enthusiastic purchaser of biographies, my mother now ordered them from the public library. Her old artist friends, Kathleen Browne and Marian Kratochwil, came each week with a cake. Marian had never forgotten my parents' kindness to him when he had arrived penniless in England forty-five years earlier, with the remnants of the Polish Army. Most weekends my parents either lunched with me or with my sister in south London.

Six months passed without a crisis, and my sister and I were starting to live our lives again, without wondering when the next alarming phone call might come. My sister took my mother to buy some new clothes, which made her look more like her old self, whenever she chose to wear them. My father settled in well, and was soon popular with the residents and staff alike.

One April evening, in the following year, I arrived at Woodstock to find my mother on edge. Before I could take her aside and ask what was the matter, my father furtively signed to me to come closer.

'She's been seeing a man, you know.'

'What sort of man?'

'Please *don't* get him started on that,' implored my mother.

'He's a little man. About five foot four,' whispered my father. 'He comes to her at night.'

'Oh yes,' groaned my mother, in her cut-glass voice, 'I get a lot of fucking these days.' I couldn't remember her ever using the word before.

A week later, 'the little man' had passed into history and my father seemed almost normal again – apart from the shuffling gait and hunched posture which went with his disease. Yet this delusionary episode depressed my mother for weeks to come, until she received another blow. The younger of the two cats she had taken into Woodstock with her – a little tortoiseshell female – had to be put down. Out of all the cats she had owned a few months ago, only Johnny Brown, her large, black, neutered tom was left.

To start with Johnny had gone out into the garden through the window and had not needed a litter tray, but after the death of his companion, my mother became increasingly possessive of Johnny, fearing that if he went out he might disappear. Nothing would change her mind – he was a vital asset and she was sticking with a stop-loss strategy.

Although I bought cat litter every week, my mother found it difficult to get down on her knees to change it. Instead she lined the tray with newspaper which quickly became saturated. I therefore paid a care assistant to deal with the litter once a day, which she did for a couple of months, until suddenly leaving Woodstock. I now learned that matron (presumably in an attempt to get rid of Johnny) was telling other members of staff not to help my mother. Fortunately, I managed to persuade another carer from a neighbouring home to take over. This arrangement worked well until the woman developed water on the knee and stopped doing the job, without a word to me. Nor did matron alert me to any problem. I did not see or smell the tray for myself, because my mother usually met me in the hall when I took her out. Nor did my sister enter my mother's room during this crucial period, since she usually arranged for her to be brought to south London in a 'Dial a Ride' taxi.

I was therefore bemused to receive, out of the blue, a letter from the chairman of Hampstead Old People's Housing Trust, asking me to remove my mother's cat within a week. I telephoned the office to remonstrate, and was summoned to an audience with this formidable, full-figured woman and two acolytes. In an attempt to lighten the atmosphere, I mentioned that thousands of cats' trays were emptied every day without any fuss, and said it wouldn't take me long to replace the sick woman. In the meantime, I promised to come twice a day to do the tray myself. Ignoring all this, the chairman simply repeated her order that I must remove the cat within seven days.

I said: 'That cat's not just an animal to her. He's a living link with her past.'

To my astonishment the woman laughed as if I'd said something amusing. 'Your mother may seem helpless to you, but she's often rude to matron and other residents.'

'Matron's the one who's rude,' I said, feeling a rush of adrenalin. 'She barged into my mother's room without knocking when I was sitting with her. She lets her run out of clean underwear.'

'I'll take this up with matron, but true or not, it won't alter the fact that your mother has said some very spiteful things to other residents.'

'I don't believe you.' I could feel my heart begin to pound.

'For your information, your mother told one poor old lady that she had inherited a lot of money and was going to buy Woodstock.'

I laughed a little wildly. 'She was joking, obviously.'

'The old lady didn't think so. A member of staff found her packing her case.'

'My mother would never have wanted her to think she had to leave. It was just a joke that went wrong. It's amazing my father's illness hasn't destroyed her sense of fun.'

'I wouldn't call it that.'

So I failed to persuade them to relent about the cat. I wondered what my mother could possibly have said to matron that might explain this hard-hearted reaction. The smell must have been bad for a few days, but it was obvious that a recurrence could be prevented. Yet before I left the office, I was told that if my mother refused to give up her cat, she herself would have to go.

I wrote to the chairman saying I would not remove Johnny myself, and added: 'Nor would it be morally or psychologically acceptable for anyone else to remove him surreptitiously. Someone in authority must tell her to her face what is going to happen. Then at a fixed date, if you have the legal right to take him, the animal will have to be taken. I will do my best to console her on both occasions.'

This letter caused a slight, but significant retreat. Since neither my sister nor I would do the deed, the chairman decided that she would not confront my mother either, on this emotionally charged matter. Rather than climb down, she passed the buck to the management committee. I was to be allowed to appeal directly to the committee's members on my mother's behalf.

I spent a tense week waiting for this meeting, and in the meantime Joyce and I looked at some other homes, in case. My mother telephoned to say that matron had just told her she 'might have to leave in a few days if she would not give up Johnny'.

'Did you try to charm her into a change of heart?'

'I told her I'd rather live in a barrel than let her take my cat.' My silence seemed to bother her. 'Might they really kick me out?'

'Of course not. Don't worry.'

In fact, the trust had the right to get rid of residents in a variety of circumstances. Matron had already invited a council health official to inspect my mother's room, so I supposed she would claim that the tray was a health hazard.

All I can clearly recall of my performance a few days later, in front of the committee, is reading out to members a newspaper article sent to me by my sister, about the benefits enjoyed by institutionalized old people who were allowed to keep pets. I felt nervous while speaking and I didn't think I'd managed to win the members over by the time I'd finished. But I was wrong to suppose these people would be as unsympathetic as the trust's three administrators.

A few days later I received a letter telling me that Johnny and my mother would be allowed to stay, on condition that I made a failsafe arrangement for cleaning his tray. This was only what common sense and humanity would have suggested to most people – and what I had already offered to do. Now, I did what I would have done a week ago had I known that the cat could stay – put up cards in newsagents. I was contacted the following day by a local woman, who was happy to come in and deal with the tray twice daily. Mary Hamilton took a liking to my mother from the beginning and would never let her down.

I had saved my mother from expulsion, much as she had once saved me. But in her case, the emotional damage would be lasting. These women should have treated my mother with understanding. Instead, they deliberately turned a simple problem into a crisis, and in the process made my mother feel a permanent misfit in her new environment. This undermined her natural optimism at the very time when my father's health was causing her unhappiness again. I would feel angry about the episode for months.

A week or so later, I came to Woodstock and was horrified to see her sitting in the hall in the chair commanding the best view of the door. Hadn't she told me to strangle her if I ever found her here? She took in my look of surprise but stared back at me without embarrassment.

'There's nothing wrong with wanting to see what's going on.'

That evening I remembered something from my childhood. Before my first term at prep school ended, I had written to my mother begging her to be on the platform when my train came in, so I wouldn't worry and would be able to leave the world of school as soon as possible.

I thought of this when I next came to take my parents out from Woodstock. My mother was watching for me in the hall, having found an adjacent chair for my father. With her coat on, and her walking stick at the ready, it was as if she could not bear to remain a second longer than she had to in this uncongenial place.

# TWELVE

Soon after my parents went to live in Woodstock, I started researching a biography of Robert Baden-Powell. After the death of his father, when little Robert was only three, his mother was tormented by the thought that he and his fatherless brothers might slip down, through poverty, into a lower social class. They were under constant pressure to please her by doing well at school, 'lest her heart grew cold'. Although *my* mother never threatened to withdraw her love, I'm sure she had similar fears for my sister and me. Our father had not died, but he was clearly too detached and other-worldly to concern himself with our advancement, on this earth anyway.

When I was a child, my mother fantasized about my joining the Royal Navy and becoming an admiral, like two of the Pasley baronets. There was still a Pasley cousin, who was an admiral, and so I was sent to see Maitland Boucher, to hear about his time as Commodore on the Murmansk convoy run.

'We never saw the Scharnhorst, just the flash of her guns in the blackness.'

He looked dogged and dependable, with a neatly clipped beard like Captain McFee's, as drawn by Edward Ardizzone in one of my favourite childhood books, *Little Tim and the Brave Sea Captain*. It was contrived that I spend a few days afloat on *HMS Tiger*, the cruiser in which Harold Wilson would later hold talks with Ian Smith, the Prime Minister of rebel Southern Rhodesia. Although I enjoyed watching the sailors getting their tots of rum, I felt sick in the Atlantic and hated the din of the ship's engines, so I was not sorry when my mother started to see merits in the Foreign Office.

'What about being a mandarin?' she asked a year later when I was fourteen.

'I've heard the FO can be rather picky these days,' I replied testily.

During my final year at Oxford, I applied for a BBC General Traineeship, which was then the corporation's only graduate entry scheme. Although my mother enjoyed watching Rupert Davies playing Maigret, she wasn't sure whether television or radio were proper careers. Nevertheless, she played an unwitting part in my interview. When I was asked what I knew of the north of England, instead of pointing out that my CV made it perfectly clear that I'd spent all my life in the South East, I told the panel that my personal 'Road to Wigan Pier' had occurred when visiting my mother after a private operation, performed in a hospital close to the famous town. The Wrightington Hospital had pioneered artificial-hip replacement and was then the only hospital in Britain carrying out the procedure. I earned some laughs with my reply, but was lucky to be offered a traineeship after giving such a misleading impression. A private operation at that date suggested greater privilege than a public school education. My mother's new hip had been paid for by my godmother, so it was absurd that I, who had lived in the smallest room in our house, surrounded by lodgers, with a father earning less than some car workers, should have represented myself as a typical rich kid for the sake of a droll answer.

Thanks to the BBC, I would soon learn a great deal about the north of England, most of it from a tough and entertaining young woman working in television Music and Arts. Joyce had grown up in working class Liverpool, and at the age of seventeen had caught a bus to London with £20 in her pocket. No heiress she. Before bringing her home, I wondered what my mother would make of her. I needn't have worried. She had always admired guts and enterprise, and treated Joyce with friendliness from their first meeting. I married Joyce in 1969, and she always got on well with both my parents.

Ten years earlier, my mother had not been so laid back. In the class-conscious 1950s, I attended dancing classes in St Saviour's Hall, just behind Harrods, to be taught the quick step and waltz by Mrs Hampshire, whose daughter, Susan, would find fame in *The Forsyte Saga*. All this was in order to enable me to go to exclusive young persons' charity dances – the first step on a ladder that might end with my getting on 'the list' of eligible men invited to the best balls of the season.

In 1956, the year of the Suez crisis, sand-coloured tanks rumbled past my school. My favourite junior master, Mr Sockett (a popular cricketer, 'Sock it to him, sir!') had been called up and was on his way to Suez already. Surely Colonel Nasser would have to bow to the might of the British Empire now? There was general incredulity when we learned that 'the greaseball' had got away with it. The father of a school friend, Sie Wilkinson, was a District Commissioner near Nairobi, so in the dormitory I learned about the Mau Mau murders. I shivered to hear that Kenya might have to be 'given up'. Faced with so much change and decline, many of my parents' contemporaries clung to their old attitudes. I think we boys did too – at any rate we listened over and over again to the escapist musical 'Salad Days', until some exasperated boy smashed the record.

When I was twelve, I became friendly at school with the Hon. Edward Gully, whose great-grandfather had been created a viscount on retiring as Speaker of the House of Commons. I wasn't aware of liking Eddie for his title, although given my mother's ambitions for me, I would be foolish to rule out subconscious influence. In fact, Eddie was far from universally respected. Though well-built and strong, he was inclined to weep when taunted – a serious defect in our eyes which cancelled out the kudos his awesome fast-bowling would otherwise have conferred.

When Eddie invited me to spend part of the summer holidays on his parents' Scottish island, my mother made discreet enquiries from an aristocratic friend who knew Veronica Selby, his mother. Although Veronica and Lord Selby were separated, my mother's informant said she was 'eccentric and a goer but thoroughly nice *au fond*'. My mother pondered what form this eccentricity might take. Was it code for drinking? If she was 'a goer', she might be 'fast', or she might simply have vitality. The Scottish island sounded fun to my mother, and she thought Lady Selby would know other landowners. Opportunities for me to meet such people were rare. So in the end, she let me go. I felt weak with excitement. I had loved *Treasure Island* and was entranced by the idea of staying on something similar. Eddie's address was in a league of its own: Shuna Castle, Shuna, Firth of Lorn. The island even had its own postage stamps.

Eddie and I travelled to London together at the end of term in the school train, then we stayed overnight at my house, before being taken to Euston by my father the following evening. On the platform, as we waited to board our sleeper, I noticed a pubic hair sticking out of my father's fly buttons, shining with a reddish glint in the evening sunlight. Determined that Eddie should not see it, I gave the hair a surreptitious yank, only to find that it was rooted securely. My father let out an audible gasp, and I gazed up at the dirty glass roof of the station, disclaiming any part in his pain. Fortunately, Eddie remained absorbed by his own thoughts.

We were already tucked up in the train, when Eddie – above me on the upper bunk – said, almost too quietly to be heard above the usual cacophony of train noises: 'I should have told you my father doesn't live on Shuna any more.'

'Bad luck,' I muttered, embarrassed by the emotion in his voice.

'Mummy has a friend,' he announced, letting this statement rest in my mind for a moment. 'His name is Donny, and he's almost a member of the family.' I was disconcerted by Eddie's awkwardness as he said this. Why should I care if his mother had a friend?

Donny turned out to be dark haired, broad shouldered, and perhaps ten years younger than Eddie's mother. I soon cottoned on to why Eddie had been embarrassed. His mother plainly doted on this 'friend', slipping her arm through his whenever she was anywhere near him, and giving him playful little kisses. With her long auburn hair and pale skin, I guessed Veronica might be attractive to other adults, but, despite this, I wasn't surprised that Donny seemed to be enduring these tributes, rather than enjoying them. He was certainly irritated by Lady Selby's insistence that we boys rise from our chairs the moment she entered the room.

'For God's sake, Veronica, don't make 'em leap about as if they've got St Vitus's Dance.'

Shuna was three-quarters of a mile across and two miles long. At the southern end were some cottages, mostly uninhabited, and at the northern extremity the castle reared up on a windswept eminence. This battlemented pile had been built by a Victorian industrialist and though only a hundred years old was falling down. The castle's electric power was by courtesy of a Heath Robinson-like generator, which made Donny swear when he tinkered with it.

The drawing room's windows afforded views of a rough lawn, dotted with islands of rhododendron and pitted with rabbit holes. Beyond the grass was a belt of woodland, and then, glinting like tarnished silver, the channel separating Shuna from the mainland. Near the centre of the mantelpiece was a framed newspaper photograph of Donny on D-Day, synchronizing his watch with other officers on a beach. This picture's prominence showed how much his military past appealed to Lady Selby. Because Veronica became emotional in the evening, generally after a few drinks, Eddie, his brother, Mike, and I, tended to amuse ourselves upstairs, away from the antlers and mock-baronial panelling.

During the day, we boys roamed about on the island, and, one afternoon, set fire to a wasps' nest inside the wheelhouse of a beached trawler. As the wasps abandoned ship in an angry cloud, I was stung on the cheek and had to run fully dressed into the sea to avoid further stings. More often, the living creatures on the island were on the receiving end. Both Mike and Eddie loved shooting rabbits, and usually left the corpses to rot where they fell, though a few were skinned and eaten. The first time I saw Eddie slit open a rabbit's stomach with his penknife and spill the palpitating intestines on the grass, I was almost sick. What would my father have said?

'Is it necessary to kill so many?' I quavered.

'God, yes. We'd be over-run otherwise. As it is, we can't have a decent lawn or grow veg.'

'You could use fences to keep them out.'

'Nothing keeps them out.' Eddie patted the twin barrels of his gun. 'Except this.' I didn't argue because I guessed he was probably right.

The slaughter often started after breakfast, so I would sneak out as soon as I woke and try to scare the rabbits away from the lawn. I never grew accustomed to the killing, especially when Mike knocked a wounded rabbit's brains out on a post, and its front paws kept moving as if it were running away. When I remonstrated, my hosts made fun of me. Shortly before I had left for Scotland, my father had torn off the day's quotation from 'The Great Thoughts Calendar' in the kitchen:

Do not be afraid of ridicule. Nine-tenths of all the bad things in the world are done because not to do them would be ridiculous.

*Leo Tolstoy*

On a hot afternoon we went up to the roof and found a thrush fluttering in a patch of tar. The stuff was drying on his chest, and the little bird was finding it harder and harder to breathe.

'We must use paraffin to clean it off,' I insisted.

Mike shook his head. 'The tar's almost dry.'

'We should still try.'

'That'd just be cruel.' Eddie sounded shocked.

Despite my pleas, Mike shot the bird at close range, leaving a pathetic scatter of blood and feathers on the roof.

Each evening we ate supper, cooked by Veronica and an island helper. To my dismay, rabbit pie was often on the menu. Lunch was usually bread and cheese, or jam – 'a piece' in the local argot. The water was peaty and the cracked china filter made little difference to its colour. In the drawing room after supper, we played backgammon with Donny. There was a wind-up gramophone in the corner and Veronica put on records: 'You're Wonderful', 'My Ideal', and of more recent vintage, 'Everything's up to date in Kansas City'. One evening, everyone got drunk on whisky and the gramophone was kept busy. Veronica's auburn hair flew as she cha-cha'd energetically, until catching her heel in the carpet and dragging Donny down on top of her. Eddie and I danced sedately with one another, often forgetting who was the woman and getting into a succession of tangles.

Next day, Lady Selby was in a moralistic mood. Eddie muttered, 'It's bunk', referring to something his mother had just said, and then he repeated the two words faster. 'It's-bunk, spunk', earning an angry rebuke from his mother.

'At your age I didn't know that word existed.'

Although leading an unconventional life, she plainly thought herself entitled to be treated as politely as the head-mistress of a well-conducted girls' school. Occasionally, she seemed to feel guilty about her boys, and would lavish on them more attention than either appeared to want.

When the weather was stormy on Shuna, there was no shelter from the wind and rain, which drummed against the windows for hour after hour. One evening after a wet day, Veronica drank more than usual and had a serious row with Donny in front of everyone. Being used to my parents' arguments, I wasn't shocked, though I felt sorry for Eddie. Veronica accused Donny of ingratitude and of not loving her. Donny claimed she had seduced him with money and had snared him into living with her.

'I should have started a career when I left the army, instead of lolling around here. It's not so bloody easy to get started again at my age.'

I couldn't tell whether he was angrier with himself or with her for his predicament. As the evening wore on the insults grew fiercer until Donny shouted that he'd had enough and was leaving her for good.

'I ought to have done it years ago,' he roared, slamming the door.

I got the feeling that Mike and Eddie had seen other famous exits, because though downcast, they didn't appear to be seriously worried. But when Donny left the castle wearing oilskins and carrying a suitcase, their mood changed at once. Veronica started to weep in gasping sobs. I wished that one of her sons would try to comfort her. At last Mike made a perfunctory attempt, but soon abandoned his efforts.

'I don't want to wake up in the morning,' Lady Selby moaned to no-one in particular.

When she appeared an hour later, much drunker, with unkempt hair and a shotgun in her hand, I thought Eddie would try to disarm her. Instead he and Mike backed towards the door, and I went with them. It was like a parody of the game 'Grandmother's Footsteps'. My heart began to pound as I realized how scared both boys were. As soon as we were out of the room, Mike ran to the primitive telephone outside the kitchen and turned the handle rapidly.

'Mrs Mackie?' he asked breathlessly. 'There may be a bad accident on the island. You must stop the Captain at the quay and send him back.'

Mike hung up, while the woman was still talking, and sprinted up the stairs. Eddie and I followed him into a bedroom with a stout mahogany door which Mike locked. We were all breathing hard. I realized that I wanted to pee quite badly. I used the washbasin while the brothers sat side by side on the only bed in the room. They looked dazed and very unhappy.

'Will she do anything?' I asked after a long silence.

'Not if he comes back,' said Mike.

'He will, won't he?' faltered Eddie.

I walked over to the window. There were hundreds of dead flies on the sill. The rain was still battering at the glass. I imagined Donny's boat thudding through the waves, and streams of water cascading from his oilskins. There had been white horses in the strait earlier in the day.

'This is some nice holiday for you,' muttered Eddie.

'It's worse for you.'

He nodded and then hung his head. Later, we lay on the bed in the dark – Eddie and me at one end, Mike at the other. The brothers were listening keenly – for her footsteps outside, or for a shot.

At about one in the morning, we heard a commotion in the hall. Mike unlocked our door and crept outside. He soon returned.

'Donny's back.'

'What are they doing?'

'Sitting on the stairs, holding hands.'

Eddie started to sniffle with relief.

In the morning, Donny told us that the sea had been too rough for him to row out in the dinghy to the bigger boat on its mooring.

'Why didn't you come straight back?' demanded Mike.

'I needed a break.'

'She might have shot herself.'

'Look, I'm sorry you were worried, old chap, but I never take risks with cartridges. They were all locked up.'

Perhaps to make up for the scare, Donny gave Eddie a copy of the famous Marilyn Monroe nude calendar. For the rest of the time I was on Shuna, Donny and Veronica seemed to get on better. Perhaps their volcanic relationship required periodic eruptions to release dangerous seismic tensions. Our days became calmer and more predictable. Donny organized the transport of many of the island's sheep to the mainland, and Eddie and I helped erect fencing round the quay, before driving the animals onto the boat.

The plan had always been that after I left the island, Eddie would come to Cornwall with me to stay in my parents' cottage. Perhaps because of what I'd witnessed, Eddie couldn't face seeing my parents in case I'd told them everything. But whatever his reasons, Eddie telephoned me the day after I left, to say he wouldn't be coming to stay with me after all. When he muttered a few unconvincing adult-sounding phrases about 'feeling below par', I didn't have the heart to press him to change his mind. Instead I asked another friend to stay, and sat down to write my 'thank you' letter to Lady Selby.

My mother's enthusiasm for aristocratic connections would never quite recover.

# THIRTEEN

A few months before my parents went to live in Woodstock, my father, already gravely ill, had somehow summoned up the energy to make the arrangements for his elderly girlfriend's funeral in Mortlake Cemetery. Since he could hardly have asked my mother's help, he had been obliged to spend hours on the telephone to friends and fellow members of the Order, and to write numerous letters in his spidery, sloping handwriting. There had also been the post-burial buffet to see to, and all his duties as her executor, such as paying bequests. 'The Performing Animals' Defence League (incorporating The Humane Society dealing with cruelty in Circus, Cinema, Music Hall, Zoo, Fun Fair, Rodeo, Bullfighting etc.)' was a leading beneficiary, as were other animal charities. Individuals received nominal legacies, my father's, at £200, being the largest.

Early in 1982, shortly before his brother died, my father had surprised me by announcing that Mrs Coley wanted me to visit her so she could give me something.

'Can't she give it to you,' I asked, 'so you could give it to me?'

'She wants to give it to you in person.'

'I'm not happy about it.'

'It would mean a lot to her.'

'Do you know what it is?'

'Something to do with Africa. Her father was there before the First World War.'

'I don't really want to accept anything.'

'She won't be around much longer, and it would make her feel a lot easier if you could do this.' He smiled rather forlornly. I knew he wouldn't press me again if I refused, although my decision plainly mattered a great deal to him. Since there was no need to tell my mother, surely I could cope with my resentment of this woman who had caused my mother such unhappiness during my childhood?

Mrs Coley lived in a couple of rooms in a house in Gilston Road, just off the Boltons, which, though close to Earl's Court, was too far these days for my father to walk. I helped him out of the car and we climbed the stairs to her cluttered little sitting room. The gas fire was turned up high and a smell of stale *eau de cologne* hung in the air. I did my best not to look hostile. In old age, Mrs Coley's eyes – her best feature in youth – bulged distressingly. They were a pale, fishy blue – but perhaps I made this association because 'coley' was a fish my mother's cats enjoyed. She had a heavy cold and her nose dripped when she removed the handkerchief she had been holding up to it. As my father withdrew discreetly to the window alcove, she beckoned me to an upright chair close to the sofa she was lying on.

'Your father's told you why I wanted to see you?' The same querulous tone I remembered from childhood.

'You want to give me something.'

'That's right. You see you're precious to him, so I want you to have something that's precious to me.' This made me squirm a little. She lifted a small red leather case from the table beside her and handed it to me. I opened it. Inside on a bed of dirty cream-coloured velvet was a silver medal attached to a blue, yellow-edged ribbon. 'My father won it for rescuing two black miners from the bottom of a mine-shaft. They were unconscious and he nearly died getting them out. There was gas down there.' I looked more closely at the medal and saw, under the word 'Courage', two men, one holding up a miner's lamp, the other lying on his back with a broken pick-axe by his side. There was no room on the medal for the second victim. She said: 'It's called the George Cross now, but it used to be the Edward Medal. They changed its name in the last war.' I could hear the sound of her wheezing above the hiss of the fire.

My father came and looked at the medal. 'What a wonderful thing, Joy. The only medal I'd like to win is for saving life.'

'Your father was a brave man,' I told her, stating the obvious.

'You've written about Africa, so these may interest you.' She thrust an envelope at me. I took out some crumpled photographs of the presentation of the medal and several letters to Mr F. H. Edgelow, her father, from the Administrator of Rhodesia.

'These do look interesting, Mrs Coley. I'll keep them with the medal.'

Just before my father and I left, Joy Coley said to me very quietly, knowing that my father was a little deaf: 'I could tell you plenty about your dear father if I wanted. Plenty.' I was shaken by this sudden flicker of malice, with my father standing just feet away. She blew her nose into her sodden handkerchief and smiled wanly at me. 'But why would I want to spoil things?'

Going down the stairs I realised I would probably never have another chance to ask her what she'd meant. But since she'd obviously been hinting at sexual activities, I could hardly have questioned her in front of my father.

'Well! What do you think of that?' asked my father happily, indicating the little box in my hand.

'It's definitely special.'

'I'll say. There can't have been many whites in Rhodesia at that date who'd have risked their lives for a couple of blacks. I'm so glad you took it. I could see how pleased she was.'

As my father stumbled from step to step beside me, I held his arm. I didn't really blame Mrs Coley for her needling remark. Guilt over the harm she'd done my mother probably explained her grand gesture. But at the last moment, her resentment of me had been too great. If I had not been born, my father would probably have left my mother for her in 1945.

So what was the truth about my father's relationship with Mrs Coley? Years later, my memory of her malevolent little dig led me to look through my father's papers with a view to answering this question.

On 15 February 1944, he wrote in his diary: 'Everything I needed Joy gave me this night.' But my father was not like most men, and what he needed might have been spiritual rather than physical. 'Joy and I need the same religious nourishment and can only obtain it together,' he wrote in 1946, before describing their closeness as 'a thing of the spirit'. At this time my father was unhappy and harassed. A new child had increased his domestic responsibilities, he was bored by his job, and Sir Thomas was still living in the family home. To make matters worse, my father had begun to doubt the Order's teachings. His friendship with Joy must therefore have provided much needed comfort at a very bleak time.

Then, in the summer of 1947, he suddenly decided that their meetings must cease. I don't know why – though it's possible he felt guilty because they were sleeping together. 'I feel the weight of my sin,' he wrote in his diary early that year, and there are other references to 'my sin' at this time. In any case, he was starting to believe that 'earthly craving' of all kinds was harming his spiritual development. He dreamt he saw 'a super being' blocking the mouth of a cave he wanted to enter. Suddenly, this 'being', now called God, produced three swords and began to slice through the rock to stop my father approaching. Away from the forbidden cave, my father was aware of 'a man being courted alternately by two women – one fair and one dark'. Mrs Coley was fair, my mother dark. The man danced with one of them 'so close as to be almost one'. Perhaps this dream suggested to my father why God might be dissatisfied with him and what the cave might symbolize.

'How can this situation be resolved?' my father wrote on a sheet of paper headed: Facts in Relation to Joy Coley. 'While I remain intact at home, how can she be done justice to? Perhaps there is no answer except that God is to be served first . . . My guide must be whether I have sacrificed enough, and this will be revealed in my conduct.' He was moving closer to thinking that 'the great questions are not to be solved by a man's thinking, only by <u>his right doing</u>'. Joy Coley did not deny that he had obligations to my mother, and to my sister and me, but added: 'I believe love is the only real obligation and that can't be set aside without disaster.' She then argued for a *ménage à trois*. My father turned this down at once, knowing the dusty response it would have got from my mother.

But Joy Coley was determined to cling on: 'Will you really be happier if you and I have no contact at all? Or perhaps we can be friends only?' In another letter she dismissed 'relationships in thought only' as 'nebulous and unworkable'. She accused him of bringing about 'the death of all that was beautiful and true in us both. I don't believe God desires such sacrifice if it does not lead to real peace and harmony.' She then left a seed in his mind that would grow. 'Nothing softens the dreadful feeling around my heart . . . I <u>must</u> have experienced this love for you in past lives, or how could I feel so intensely?'

The Order's founder believed that incidents in past lives could be 'recovered' through dreams, and when my father started to have dreams in which he hurt Mrs Coley, he decided she had been right to think they had loved and harmed one another in previous incarnations. Her unhappy letters made him feel callous for not seeing her. He wrote in his diary: 'Perhaps I could agree to see her once in a while? Would this be a violation of family claims? Would it be wise? Would it be the will of God?' At last, in June 1951, he decided that it *could* be permitted. Because of his and Joy's past 'history', they were destined, he thought, to live out the legacy of old lives in this present one.

My father only agreed to resume occasional meetings on condition that the friendship was platonic. Even if their relations had been sexual in 1946 and 1947, he definitely kept his later resolution to be chaste. I found some of Joy Coley's diaries among my father's papers, and in them she often bemoaned his failure to reciprocate. 'If he had only met my love, I could have been so much more to him, but alas he did not want it . . . If only we could have lived together in every way, and led the practical spiritual life that would have fulfilled us both.'

My father did what he thought was honourable by staying married to my mother, by being an active father, and by continuing to see Mrs Coley rather than abandon her. He sacrificed his own and Joy Coley's happiness, but I doubt he would have been much happier if he had lived apart from his wife and children. I never got the feeling that he thought he had made a dreadful mistake, though I may be wrong about this.

While my father had been struggling with the arrangements for Joy Coley's funeral, my mother said she would like to be taken to West End, in Surrey, so she could finally decide whether she wanted to be buried close to her parents. As we were driving over Putney Bridge, she asked whether I had any thoughts on the subject. I said that if *my* father had cut me out of his will, I wouldn't be keen to be buried anywhere near him. And talking of my father – would he want to spend eternity beside his father-in-law? I thought her silence meant she'd dismissed what I'd said, but then she muttered:

'Maybe he should go to his family plot in Dorking.'

'I expect he'd much rather be buried with you.'

It was a wet and dreary afternoon with slow-moving rain clouds overhead. Heavy drips fell from overhanging trees as we entered the graveyard. My mother stood for a long time leaning on her stick at her parents' grave, while I held an umbrella over her. The cross was tilting slightly and weeds had sprouted between the gravel chippings.

I said: 'One would have thought the Gordon Boys might have looked after the grave.'

My mother simply sighed and said she would like to look at her mother's window in the chapel. When we found the building locked, she asked to be taken to the school. I drove her into an asphalted yard with a lawn on one side and low redbrick buildings around us. A few boys walked past the car, whistling tunelessly. They were either wearing utilitarian overalls or nondescript jerseys and flannel trousers.

'Their uniform used to be tartan trousers and glengarries,' she told me. 'Gordon tartan for everything, including the ribbons.'

'If you'd like to visit the house you used to live in, I expect I could find someone who . . .'

'Please don't do that. I've seen enough.'

As we drove slowly past the graveyard, an old man was coming out – a gardener I guessed from his clothing. He couldn't be a gravedigger at his age. My mother tapped my arm.

'Let me talk to him.'

We stopped and she wound down her window. 'Do you remember when Sir Thomas Pasley was Commandant at the Home?'

The old man took off his cap and smoothed his white hair. 'That'd be a long while back. Things were different then all right.'

'They certainly were,' said my mother.

'We had the future King visit us.'

'I was there.'

'Who were you then, if you don't mind telling?'

My mother surprised me by laughing, 'Then? Oh, I was someone else entirely.' The gardener looked at her a little reproachfully. She managed a smile. 'I was little Norah Pasley.'

When we were driving back towards London through sandy heathland, my mother said: 'I used to catch the last train home when I was singing in London. Father always insisted on sitting up for my cab. He hated me working in town.' Then she turned to me with a lovely spontaneous smile that seemed to come straight from her happier past. 'It would be an awful waste of everyone's time to come all this way, twice.' I must have looked puzzled. 'Once for your father and once for me.'

'I wouldn't have minded if it was what you wanted.'

'What'd be the point? I'd rather you found somewhere for us in London.'

My sentimental self wanted to beg her to change her mind, but her jaw was set in a way I knew well. She'd had the guts to see things as they really were. So why should I plead for self-deception? It would have been monstrous for her to be buried in a place where her father had destroyed her singing career, when she had been 'someone else entirely'.


In the summer of 1984, two years after my parents had moved to Woodstock, I was still in the midst of researching my biography of Baden-Powell, who despite many virtues turned out to have enjoyed dancing in a skirt, watching executions, and looking at photographs of naked men and boys. As well as searching for letters and diaries, I met surviving friends, colleagues and family members.

That July, I went to Walsingham in Norfolk to see eighty-five-year-old Claude Fisher, Baden-Powell's press officer during the 1920s. When I arrived, he was not in his room in the religious care home where he lived, but had gone out into the town to avoid me – though he had agreed to be interviewed. Walsingham is not large and I ran him to earth in a street near the shrine, among the pilgrims and liturgical shops. He was stumbling along over the cobbles, pushing a wheeled walking frame. His appearance was mole-like, eyes half-shut and lids crusted with scabs. His feet, inside special sandals, were bandaged, leaving visible his gnarled, yellow toenails. He was not repentant. Yes, he *had* said he would see me, but he'd changed his mind and what was so bad about that?

'The man's dead and buried, like I will be soon enough. No-one understands what it was like back then, and it's a waste of time trying to tell people. Just leave us all alone, can't you.'

Without another word he began pushing his walking frame away from me. A procession of pilgrims emerged from the shrine and swept him along with them, out of my sight. Curmudgeonly old people like Claude made me wonder whether, like him, my mother would one day stop believing in the value of her own life, and therefore in the lives of others.

I dropped in on my parents the following evening. My mother asked how my work was going, more for form's sake I felt, than out of genuine interest. She had been sitting in the garden a lot recently, and her face was the same dark brown I'd previously associated with the faces of vagrants. What did she think about, sitting out there for hours on end?

During my visit – tactfully waiting till my mother was briefly out of the room – my father questioned me about 'the fish market at the end of the corridor'. Why should this particular delusion have proved so enduring? As a couple, my parents could still reinforce each other's sense of their old identity, but this would no longer be possible when one partner finally moved into a different mental world. My mother had long been dreading this.

Stoicism is a style that is said to insulate its practitioners from the intolerable nature of their situation; and to some extent I think it helped my mother. She had always instructed me not to cry in front of anyone, and now she didn't ring me up to moan about her plight. Nor did she ever weep again in front of me, as she had done outside the hospital. She was developing a raffish and slightly negligent persona, wearing skirts that were clearly not meant to go with particular blouses, and affecting odd-looking hats, ranging from an immense straw one to a droopy woollen beret.

At about this time, she suffered from severe toothache. Her usual dentist was away, so I took her to the emergency dental unit at University College Hospital. For weeks she had been using whisky to dull the pain in her front teeth. The emergency dentist examined her, took x-rays, and then explained apologetically that he couldn't save these conspicuous teeth. My mother waved a regal hand.

'Yank 'em out; I'm not Brigitte Bardot.'

Afterwards, holding a bloody cloth to her mouth, she accompanied me to the car.

'You were very gutsy in there.'

'Don't give me that. I hardly felt a thing, and, anyway, who cares what I look like. *I* certainly don't.'

Compliments and all tactful circumlocutions were rejected by her from now on. Her life gave her little fun, and she was determined that there should be no pretences to the contrary. Considering how much she had enjoyed her pleasures in the past, the change was painful to witness. At least her lost teeth led to flashes of her old humour. When she next visited my house, she tantalized my children by opening and shutting her mouth so quickly that they couldn't quite see the devastation within. When her false teeth arrived, she kept them up her sleeve and only brought them out to snap together like a curious castanet. It also amused her to make her jaw creak like the hinge of an ancient chest, making the children shriek with horrified admiration. Perhaps my mother's increasingly gruff and unpredictable manner helped her work off some of her frustration.

To what extent she took refuge in an idealized past, I don't know, but one afternoon, she fished out an old Irish newspaper, *The King's County Chronicle*, containing several flowery and sycophantic columns on the front page, devoted to her parents' wedding. My mother also produced from the

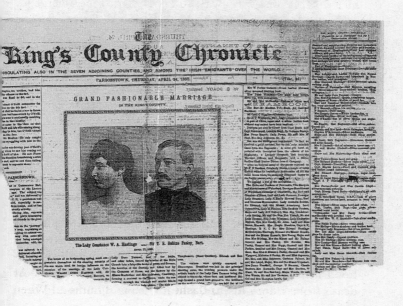

same wooden box a photograph of the rich and titled folks on the lawn, while above them on a balcony, servants lolled in attitudes of satirical indifference – the photographer having neglected, perhaps deliberately, to trim them out of the picture. In her room in Woodstock, my mother had placed photographs of my sister and me and her grandchildren all around her, but a picture of her own mother, circa 1890, wearing on her head an amazing confection of silk and feathers, had pride of place on the table by her bed.

'Now *she* was nice', my mother told me, gazing at her mother's face. My mother's only sister had died thirty years earlier and so there was nobody alive who shared her childhood memories. My mother's mother had suffered a slow death from kidney disease, and for many months had been unable to attend sports days, parades and royal visits to the Gordon Boys' Home. Instead, on special occasions, she had sat propped up in her bedroom window to gaze at what was going on. As a child, my mother had often seen nothing of her parents until the end of the day, when she'd been summoned to the dinner table to eat a few nuts with them, and have a sip of port.

Through remembering her old life with pride, my mother underpinned her sense of her own significance. This was the reverse of how my father dealt with adversity. In his opinion, pride was the great obstacle to man's union with God, so he thought his best hope of coming to terms with misfortune lay in seeing himself, humbly, for what he really was.

Earlier in the day, my father had been struggling with a letter to a Mr Fryer about his subscriptions to a magazine called the *Crusader,* connected with the Nature Cure Clinic. Since his draft was almost illegible, I offered to type it. He had headed it: Woodstock, Old People's, 37 Elsworthy Road, NW3. 'Many thanks for your recent letters. I have had a dose of PARKINSON'S DISEASE, and I am still in hospital (out patients) & on drugs. But am glad to be able to make some progress.' The letter had then dealt with the subscriptions. I realised what a great effort it must have cost him to write this brief letter, and I found it very moving that he should have said he was making 'some progress' – his characteristic optimism seeming more poignant precisely because the truth was so different. I also wrote a reply to someone called Ethne-Iris Payne, who had been on the Nature Cure Clinic Committee with him. 'Dear Clifford, I keep thinking of you, & wondering how you've been since I saw you at the Annual General Meeting in '82. I still miss you, we all do at the meetings . . .'

That evening I had what would turn out to be one of the

last coherent conversations I can remember having with my father. He chose to talk about the happy times we had had when he and my mother had taken me out from prep school. Often we had had picnics at Fairlight beach on the East Sussex coast.

'What a staggering place – as if the sand stretched to the edge of creation.' My father paused to look at me. 'When *you* visit such places, don't you feel sad not to belong to them?'

'I don't really understand you.'

'Have you never felt hungry – homesick almost – for some perfect place that lies just beyond what you're actually seeing?'

'I love wild places; but to be honest, what I see is enough.'

He squeezed my hand. 'It'll happen for you one day. I know it will.'

I clearly remembered one visit to Fairlight with my parents. Their friend, Harry, had come, and two school friends of mine. After eating a picnic, I ran with them on that immense beach, racing on for ages across the wet sand, like prisoners on a spree, intoxicated by the unfamiliar experience of freedom. Recalling that day, I felt very close to the person my father had been then. A few months later I would have given a lot to have a similar chat with him. I had brought some greengages and a peach, which I now cut up for him.

'What a peach of a peach,' he murmured, savouring the aftertaste.

Whenever I said goodnight to my father these days, he smiled broadly as he stretched out under the sheets and relaxed. It comforted me that he could still feel physical contentment despite his illness. I thought: if only things can go on like this for a little longer.

But within two months his Parkinson's had grown more debilitating, with constant tremor in his right hand, greater difficulty in getting moving and considerable deterioration of his mental state. This decline was an established trend when, one warm afternoon in mid-September, I took my two younger daughters to Woodstock. My parents were in the garden on the edge of the lawn. My father was not sitting on the same bench as my mother, and he looked hunched up and frail. He was wearing a small straw-hat that reminded me slightly of a wastepaper basket. At least he was in a good position to watch Lucy and Emily as they began to rush about on the grass. Emily, then five, was laughing and shrieking as her ten-year-old sister caught up with her and gave her little pushes. Emily had tightened her Alice band so that it thrust her hair upwards like a hedgehog's quills. Lucy's long blond hair was streaming out behind her. It was lovely to see them so animated. I was saying something to my mother, when Lucy called out to me:

'Dad! Come quickly! Grandpa's running!'

To my amazement my father had got up from his bench and was running across the lawn. I couldn't believe what I was seeing. With his weight pitched forward as if sprinting in a race, he dashed on for almost twenty yards, somehow managing to slow down before reaching the rose beds. I ran towards him, scared he might fall, but he reached the bench almost nonchalantly, as if this were the sort of thing he did all the time.

'How on earth did you do *that*?' I gasped.

'They were having such fun, I thought I'd join in.'

In my memory, this moment merges with others: my father running in Kensington Gardens to get my kite to fly; sprinting in the fathers' race at my prep school; doing his Chinese exercises with perfect physical control.

# FOURTEEN

In 1985, Jessica, our eldest daughter was working for her
'O' Levels. The walls of her room were covered with posters
advertising pop groups: Redskins, The Clash, Madness, The
Damned, and there was also a large collage made up of
photographs of macho-looking boys. She was our first

teenager, and Joyce and I may have erred on the side of caution when insisting we must always speak to the parents of party-givers who had invited her. This was after she told us, perhaps unwisely, that the parents of a friend had returned home late one evening to find a party in progress and their home wrecked. The parents had then been knocked about by their daughter's uninvited 'guests'. But in general, Jessica's adolescence was a pre-drugs, pre-raves idyll. To be telephoned a few times at two or three in the morning, and be asked to fetch a daughter from some distant suburb is nothing much to complain about.

Shortly before my fortieth birthday, Jessica got herself a punk haircut and a boyfriend with a tall orange Mohican crest on his shaved head. One night he and she woke us all in the small hours. I was enraged. The next morning I found (in illustration of one of my mother's favourite maxims, 'never judge a sausage by its skin') that he had left me a highly literate and amusing note of apology.

In Jessica's exam year, Joyce and I were also thinking about Lucy, and were wondering whether she should go to a music school or to an ordinary secondary one. I mentioned our quandary to my musically gifted mother.

'I haven't the faintest idea what you should do,' she told me, 'and even if I did know, I'd be a fool to say.'

'Why's that?'

'With my luck it would probably turn out to be all wrong for her.' My mother gave me what I was coming to recognize as her twisted smile. 'If your father's right about reincarnation, I must have done something very wicked in a past life to deserve the life I have now.'

In March 1985, when she was ten, I drove Lucy to the Menuhin School near Cobham in Surrey for her audition. It was probably anxiety rather than car sickness that made her beg to be let out of the car in Cobham High Street. Either way, she was sick in the gutter and I had to hurry off to buy a bottle of water and some tissues to clean up her shoes. Inevitably, it had occurred to Joyce and me – neither of us being musicians – that Lucy's violin teacher might have deluded herself into thinking her more talented than she was. With musical children coming for audition from all over the world, I wondered if we should have exposed her to this stressful situation.

The school was a large Victorian mansion at the end of a drive, housing roughly sixty young musicians between ten and eighteen. Each pupil had a bedroom containing a practice piano. It was like entering a world incredibly remote from the workaday one we had just left. Parents and candidates were asked to wait in a large ground-floor room, where I was struck by the number of Japanese and Korean candidates and by the extraordinary neatness of their clothing. Every pleat and crease in every tartan dress or pair of trousers had been meticulously pressed. Time dragged by. Candidate followed candidate from the room, the heavy door closing with a thump behind each, until at last Lucy's name was called. I tried to read a book when she had gone, but failed. My nervousness had little to do with whether Lucy might eventually be admitted to this rarefied place. I was worrying about how she would feel if rejected.

When Lucy finally came out I could tell nothing from her face. She said she thought it had gone reasonably well, although she had cried at one point.

'Why was that?'

'I don't want to talk about it, dad.'

Since I had expected to hear from the school by letter, I was surprised to get a telephone call a few hours after returning to London. Lucy had impressed everyone with her playing – even her tears had found favour as evidence of a passionate nature.

I was told that two Chinese pupils had been summoned home at short notice, so there were two vacancies at the school now. Would Lucy like to take up one of these places at once, rather than wait to enter the school at the usual time with the new entrants in September? I promised to discuss the offer with her.

I told my mother about the audition the following day, and she listened politely but made no comment except that I must be proud. Maybe Lucy's talent brought back painful memories of her own career. After a few days, Lucy decided she did not want to go to the Menuhin School. With only a handful of students of exactly her age, what would happen if she were to fall out with a few? About a month later, Lucy auditioned at the Purcell School, a larger music school, with more day pupils than boarders and a broader mix of abilities. When offered a scholarship, she accepted it.

In 1985, all my children were stepping out into new worlds – Emily our youngest included, since she had just gone to primary school. In this same period, my parents' horizons seemed by contrast to be contracting. Absorbed by my father's accelerating decline, my mother's inquiries about her grandchildren became fewer as the months passed.

Even after my father's confusion grew worse, he still enjoyed visiting my home, smiling at the children and at Joyce, before kneeling to stroke our golden retriever, Boz, and our marmalade cat, Tigger. Then, with Boz's head resting on his leg, he would lie on the floor to relax.

My father had been relaxing in the same way since 1946, when he had noted in his diary: 'King's Langley relaxation technique. Wonderful in its effects. It came with utter and complete opportuneness when I was at the end of myself, at point of zero.' The technique involved lying flat on the floor and going through a routine of deep breathing, and conscious 'letting go', while thinking of 'some beautiful, happy scene associated with early life such as the view from Leith Hill'. 'Once you get that feeling of peace; just let it come in,' he told his brother in a letter. 'The mind is filled with emptiness. Then the soul is ready for an influx of the Divine Spirit . . .'

On a sunny day in May 1985 – which also happened to be one of his good days – Joyce and I took him and my mother to Lewes, in Sussex, to see one of the two women who had played for my mother during her singing career. Val Longhurst was in her late seventies now but had remained active and youthful. She had been a violinist as well as a pianist, and she still played the piano for regular violin pupils.

Now Val accompanied Lucy in works by Bach, Dvorak and Mozart. On the far side of the room, my father was lying on the floor relaxing. I was sitting with Joyce, with my back to him. Suddenly I heard a gasp and spun round. His hands were raised as though to embrace some invisible object, floating above his chest. My mother was staring at him with mortification and dismay.

'The light of lights,' he gasped joyfully. 'It's all around me.'

'What on earth's he saying?' demanded my mother.

'Such happiness for everyone,' sighed my father, and then something scarcely audible about 'warmth'.

Hoping to keep my mother quiet, I whispered: 'I think he's having a religious experience.'

'Having *what*?' she demanded, like some scandalized Lady Bracknell. Lucy had stopped playing and was gazing at grandpa too. My mother favoured me with her twisted smile: 'Your father certainly chooses his moments.'

He was still lying in the same position, a faint smile on his lips, when Lucy and Val resumed their playing.

Before we left, I helped my father to the lavatory. When he had finished peeing, I lowered the lid so he could sit on it.

'What happened just then?' I asked.

'It was like being flooded with the brightest light you can possibly imagine.'

'Where was this light?'

'In the room but in me too – I can't say exactly where in my body. I think I *was* the light for a while.' His eyes filled with tears. 'How poor words are.'

Had this been his long awaited moment of 'Oneness with God'? I wanted to ask him, but didn't dare in case it had not been what he'd longed for. It had been something remarkable anyway, I told myself.

About seven years earlier, before my father's illness had been diagnosed, I drove my parents to Kent to visit the widow of one of my father's oldest friends. She lived in Deal, in a picturesque side-street, about fifty yards from the beach. After lunch my father said he was going to swim and urged me to come too. I followed him out of the house, but reluctantly since I disliked the pebbly beach that sloped steeply into the sea.

In my early twenties I had been swept out to sea from a beach near Mullion in Cornwall, and although I managed to reach the shore several coves away, the experience had left me scared of offshore currents. My father knew this, but never changed his habit of swimming out for half-a-mile or more and then floating on his back for a long time. It was inconceivable to him that water – the element he loved so much, both physically and symbolically – could ever harm him. On our previous visit to Deal, he'd conceded that the Cornish coast could be dangerous, but Kent was quite different, he'd insisted, before persuading me to swim. Today I stood firm, though I knew he was disappointed. I had no premonition that I was turning down what would turn out to have been our last chance to swim together.

The beach at Deal might have been designed by a creator eager to test the courage of swimmers with bad feet. The stones slipped about because of the slope of the beach, and were just the size to cause my father maximum discomfort. But like some salmon returning to its spawning ground, he struggled seaward, upright at first, then creeping on hands and knees to save the soles of his feet. The moment the water was up to his knees, he dived forward vigorously, and in seconds was swimming away with that effortless crawl. Soon he was no more than a tiny dot, way out to sea.

Perhaps foolishly, I had come to share his confidence that he would never drown. Yet today I found myself thinking of those well-known lines from *The Tempest*:

> Full fathom five thy father lies;
> Of his bones are coral made;
> Those are pearls that were his eyes:
> Nothing of him that doth fade,
> But doth suffer a sea-change
> Into something rich and strange.

The sea really *did* change my father, giving him back the grace and ease of movement he had enjoyed years earlier but had lost on land. He had written long ago: 'Be not merely in the river, but become part of it, through its penetration of one's whole Being.' And 'part of it' was what he always seemed to be when he swam. In the same notebook, he asked: 'Is some part of me undying?', and answered, 'Not some part of me, but something I am part of, <u>God's life-stream, the living water</u>' (his underlining).

One sunny afternoon in August 1985, three months after our trip to Val's house in Lewes, I took Lucy with me to Woodstock. We went straight to my mother's room, but she was not there. Johnny eyed us suspiciously from her bed. The room was untidy because my mother was endlessly taking books from her shelves and forgetting to put them back. On every available surface there was an accumulating mess of old envelopes and scraps of paper on which she had written reminders to herself and telephone numbers – often Thomasina's and mine. On her needlework stool was a pile of newspapers over a foot deep.

Supposing that my mother was in the garden with my father, we left her room, glancing in at my father's as we passed. I was shocked to see him sitting in here on this lovely day. He'd been finding it increasingly difficult to focus on actual things, and leaving him alone like this was not going to help him look outward. His was the only chair, so Lucy and I sat beside him on the bed. After a period of almost death-like inactivity, he said:

'Did you do anything spectacular yesterday afternoon?'

'What did you have in mind?' I asked, amused despite my sadness to find he'd been left inside.

Another long silence persisted. At last my father sighed: 'Years ago they lost touch . . . the brothers.' He opened his eyes but they were unseeing, still focused inwards. 'There were two brothers,' he added, placing himself, as well as Ted, firmly in the past.

Quite often recently, I had heard my father speak of himself in the third person. He seemed almost to be taking leave of himself. It was awful to see his personality fading away like the image in some old photograph, giving us no chance to mourn or even mark this series of imperceptible deaths.

When I went to ask the matron why he had not been taken out into the garden, I thought Lucy had followed me. Ten minutes later, I went back and found her still sitting with her grandfather, keeping him company.

* * *

During the autumn of 1985, the staff at Woodstock ceased to be able to take care of my father. Mary, one of the care assistants, had always been kind and patient. I still have a 'get well' card she wrote that summer after my parents had recovered from heavy colds. 'To Dear Mr and Mrs Jeal . . . I do hope you are both well now. My love to you both always, Mary (Your Nurse) xxx.' But now, there could be no denying the fact that my father could not manage the stairs up to the ground floor. One day, he refused to eat or be fed. The new West Indian matron, whom I found very sympathetic, told my mother and me that she thought he was telling us he wanted to die.

'I'm afraid he'll have to be admitted to the Royal Free.'

My mother looked puzzled. 'But *they* won't let him die, will they?'

'We can't either.'

'Even though he has no chance of getting better?'

Matron said gently: 'In hospital they'll be able to look after him better than we can. They'll make him stronger, improve his walking. It's amazing what they achieve.'

'If only they could improve his mind,' sighed my mother.

'He'll have to concentrate when he's with the physio people. That may help his mind. I've known cases where it has.'

After matron had gone, my mother said to me: 'Wouldn't it be nice if she was right.'

I went in to see my father a week after his admission to the Royal Free. Before this visit, my mother had told me – much to my surprise, since only days ago she had seemed in favour of letting him die – that she missed him a great deal.

'The two of us go back such a long way.'

'I do understand.'

She shook her head vehemently. 'You don't really. How can you? You never knew him as he was before we married. He was so handsome, and so loving until the religious bug bit him.'

I drove the short distance to the hospital in the car, listening on the way to an actor reading an excerpt from a surreal novel in the 'magical realism' school. I guessed that no member of this writer's family had suffered hallucinations for any length of time.

From across Malcolm Ward, I could see that my father's hair had been cut. Before his admission it had been long and wispy, and I found its current tidiness superficially reassuring. As I approached, my father stared hard. Was I, or was I not, someone he ought to know? To my relief, when I was a yard or two away, he gave me a definite smile of recognition. I saw at once that he was holding his head up better, and that his upper body was less stooping. His dribbling – one of the least attractive side-effects of his medication – was also less noticeable. In contrast to his introversion at Woodstock, he looked around a lot, his attention caught by the activities of nurses and cleaners.

He turned to a nurse who was making the bed opposite. 'You're busy this-morning,' he said in a normal conversational tone.

'Don't tell me,' she laughed.

'But you're keeping abreast of things,' he reassured her.

'Just about.'

After this, he talked to me about some gold shares his brother had once recommended, and about Ted himself. Slightly encouraged, I asked him if he remembered my name, but he closed his eyes as if too tired to answer.

I had recently been gripped by the idea that a brain active enough to enable its owner to read could not be on the verge of extinction. To find out whether he still had the ability, I had brought a book belonging to Emily. It was called *Kevin the Kitten* – a choice I hoped he wouldn't find insulting, but it seemed logical to start with something printed in large type. After persuading my father to put on his reading glasses, I handed him this small book.

'Please will you read some of it out loud?'

I waited nervously while he stared at one of the illustrations, before glancing at the text. 'Kevin put some water in a bucket,' he intoned mechanically, and then went on to despatch another sentence in the same flat, uninvolved tone. Although I was delighted by my discovery, I couldn't pretend that the remote way in which he had read had been very hopeful. Mere words seemed to leave no mark in his mind.

I moved closer to him. 'You can read perfectly well. So would you like your Order of the Cross books?' He shook his head in a clear gesture of rejection, and then closed his eyes. Believing he would make no further attempt to talk to me, I got up to go. At that moment, he opened his eyes and looked at me directly for the first time. To my amazement, I felt that he was really seeing me.

'The living water,' he said very distinctly – his eyes still fixed on mine. I felt he was making a supreme effort to reach out to me from deep inside himself. Then he repeated the same words in a slightly more inward tone. This time too, his delivery was markedly different from the detachment that had coloured everything else he had said.

Going down in the lift, I felt sure that he had just told me something of great importance to himself. I remembered him crawling towards the sea at Deal, as if drawn to it. And that phrase from his writings returned to me: 'God's Lifestream, the living water.' Behind closed lids, did he already imagine himself seaward bound?

I drove straight from the hospital to see my mother in Woodstock, arriving as it was getting dark. She was wearing an old green dressing gown over her clothes, although her electric heater was blowing out heat into the already stifling air. I began to tell her about my discovery that my father could read.

'That's not much use,' she sighed. 'He never looks at anything.'

'But if he can recognize words, his brain can't be as bad as we thought.'

'If he doesn't use it, what difference does it make?'

'Maybe even when he sounds scrambled, he's understood what's been said to him. Before I left, he said something special.'

'Really?' She didn't try to hide her scepticism.

'You know how he loved the sea and swimming. Well just as I was leaving, he said: "The living water." It was like saying he was all right deep inside.'

My mother's answer was a scarcely perceptible shrug. 'When Thomasina visited him on Monday, he didn't know her from Eve. He seemed more interested in the staff than in her.' My mother's eyes met mine: 'Tell me honestly if you think he'll ever come back here.'

'It's too early to tell.'

Her old black cat jumped onto her lap. She stroked him gently and he started to purr. 'If I didn't have Johnny, I'd go raving mad.'

It occurred to me that since Johnny was about fourteen, he might die any day. But then so might my mother. She had not put in her teeth today, and their absence made her cheeks appear shrunken. Every time I saw her these days, I suffered the delusion that she had become smaller. Yet she remained such a brave, obstinate little person.

\* \* \*

That evening I read Emily her bedtime chapter of *The Wickedest Witch in the World*. Afterwards, she looked at me intently and asked: 'Why am I me, daddy?'

'I don't know, Em. It's tied up with having lots of memories of earlier in your life. And having your own brain and no one else's.'

'But why aren't I someone else?'

'I've no idea.'

Memory was what conferred identity, more than anything. So who was my father now?

A few days earlier Emily had told me that she and her school friend, Kate, would be going to fairyland soon and that, on arriving there, she would make sure that Joyce and I stopped getting any older. Her grandfather's fate must have made her eager to spare us something similar. As for herself, the fairies would let her stay the same age for as long as she wanted. About two months earlier, I had found Emily weeping over some photographs taken of her and her best friend, Amy, when they'd both been younger. I'd tried to persuade her that she was gaining more by growing up than she was losing. Wasn't she enjoying her new school, making friends, doing far more for herself? But she wasn't convinced.

Earlier in the year, Joyce and I had thought we might move to a slightly larger house. To judge whether this would be possible or not, we had put our house on the market to see what offers we received. When potential buyers came to the house, Emily lurked on the stairs so she could announce in their hearing that this was her home and that she didn't want anyone to buy it. She felt that everything ought to stay the way it was, and we shouldn't even think about moving to some house that wasn't our proper home. Everything was right the way it was now. Joyce and I loved to watch Emily pottering about, drawing and painting, stroking the cats and the dog, playing with her friends, chatting with her sisters, completely content with her childhood, as time slept for her.

The idea of selling the house was gradually abandoned, and not just because of Emily. While coping with the existential chaos caused by unreliable chemical messengers in the brain of a much loved family member, it seemed wiser to hang on to what was familiar, than to seek out unnecessary change.

# FIFTEEN

Two weeks after my previous visit to the Royal Free, I took my mother to see my father. It worried me that on one level she was looking forward to seeing him, even if on another she was telling herself not to hope at all. Recently, my mother had been finding it harder to walk and would let out little groans as she climbed the steps up to my front door when visiting me. Even when crossing from her bed to the chair in her room, she would emit an occasional gasp, as if the process of moving even this short distance was too much for her. So it was a relief to me when she decided to allow me to push her in a wheelchair along the hospital's long and soulless corridors. There was another advantage too – when the lifts appeared, she would not be able to make a tottering rush towards whichever appeared first, regardless of whether it was going up or down.

My father was not in bed, but sitting in a wheelchair in a side ward. As soon as we reached him it was all too clear that he was much worse than a week ago. For a start, he had been put on a catheter and there was a bag of discoloured urine hanging down beside his wheelchair. He was also dribbling more and his shirt was saturated. I must have stopped wheeling my mother closer because I suddenly heard her say: 'I can't talk to him from here.'

So I pushed her up to him. My mother leaned forward in her chair and clasped my father's left hand – his right was lying in his lap, shaking rapidly.

'Hello, Joe,' she said firmly. 'How are you today?'

My father said nothing, but looked for a moment as if he might speak. Then, apparently forgetting that there was anyone in front of him, he closed his eyes. My mother kept talking, doing her best to produce some remembered event or person that would draw him out. She even tried recalling the place where they had gone for their honeymoon. After a while, I couldn't bear to go on listening, but went to the large plate-glass window and looked at the lights of Hampstead below. From the opposite side of the building, I would have been able to see my own house, where Jessica and Lucy would probably be doing their homework or watching television, and Emily drawing at the kitchen table. How lucky I was to have this life to go back to.

When I returned to the side ward, I was amazed to see that my father was talking. Could my mother really have managed to cut through his mental fog and elicit a real response? But when I got closer, I could hear him complaining about 'Old Mr Bishop who runs the whole estate' – by which he meant some entirely imaginary manager of some mythical market-garden, supposed to be 'across the road from Woodstock'. My mother was upset and drained. Seeing her sunk low in her wheelchair, beside my gaunt and uncomprehending father, was one of the saddest sights I'd ever seen.

I went to say my own goodbye to him. 'I'm going now, daddy.'

His face was absolutely immobile and I expected no further

response, but suddenly – just as had happened on my last visit – he opened his eyes and seemed against all odds to reach out to me from an immense distance. My mother was too distressed to notice him, as he looked straight at me and said:

'It could be worse.'

On our way back to Woodstock in the car, I repeated what he had just said, and added: 'I think he was trying to comfort us. I honestly do.'

My mother shook her head vehemently. 'The poor man's finished. I can't bear to see him again.'

'If a miracle happens you can always change your mind.'

My mother glanced at me but forbore to comment. What had I been thinking of, babbling about miracles, when logic told me that the best we could hope for could only be a few more of his superhuman attempts to reach us through the fog of his obliterating illness?

A few days later, I drove an old artist friend of my parents down to Battle in East Sussex where she had been invited by the owner of a country hotel to spend a few weeks recuperating after an operation. It had not occurred to me in advance that our journey would take us past the gates of my old prep school. So their sudden appearance to the right of the road, struck me, just as happens in dreams, as being both extraordinary and unsurprising at the same moment. As if programmed to do so, I swung the car into the drive. It was the same place; and yet it wasn't at all. The tarmac had become potholed and overgrown, and the playing fields had simply disappeared under great banks of brambles. From a distance, the house itself looked untouched by time. Closer to, something was clearly amiss. The wing that had contained the junior classrooms and the changing rooms was no longer there.

I walked up to the open hall door and gazed in. The whole interior had been ripped apart by builders. On the very spot where my father had once embarrassed me by confessing that we had walked from the station, stood a portable shed. Inside it, I found the foreman, and learned from him that the school was being converted into flats for weekenders and City commuters. The pseudo-Jacobean coats of arms above the fireplace that I had often gazed at while the headmaster read to us on winter Sunday evenings – books such as *Moonfleet* and *Stalky and Co.* – had disappeared. Many doorways had been closed up, and other openings smashed right through outer walls. This place, which I had once thought as formidable and enduring as Colditz Castle or Alcatraz, had turned out to be just another large house that could be knocked about or even razed to the ground at the whim of some developer.

I walked up the broad stairs, on which I had often waited for my summons to be beaten, and entered the headmaster's study. The bookcases had been ripped out and all the floorboards were up. The view from the window was unrecognisable – the fir trees were gone and some of the fields had been built on. I struggled to reconcile memory with reality. I thought of the people my father and I had been on the day we had first visited this place thirty-three years earlier, and what we had subsequently become, and I was dazed by the precariousness of all personal identity. And then I thought back even earlier. If my mother had not gone shopping for modern furniture at Heal's in the Tottenham Court Road, and if my father had not been earmarked for Arnhem, I would not have had my life. And if there had been no flying bombs, my parents would never have moved to Oxford and would not have met my godmother, who would never have recommended that I come to the school that had once existed in the shell of this house. In every life there would be this same randomness.

As I drove away, the arbitrariness of my father's illness seemed a little less personally wounding. It had happened by chance, like almost everything else.

Early in 1986, I was at the point in my biography where Baden-Powell was a nineteen-year-old cavalry officer serving in Afghanistan. Two battalions of a British regiment had just been cut to pieces by tribesmen, and Lord Roberts was punishing the Afghans by hanging scores of them outside the main gate of Kandahar. A mile away, Baden-Powell was raising morale with his regimental production of 'The Pirates of Penzance' in which he played 'Little Ruth', singing in tremulous contralto and wearing a crinoline. I was recording this improbable stuff when Lucy burst into my room to summon me to a different form of unreality.

'You must come down to the hall now, dad. Hurry.'

Emily and her friend, Kate, were hovering near the door, wearing frothy ballet dresses and homemade wings which they were jiggling up and down as if about to fly away. On the floor were dozens of plastic bags containing clothes, books and food. It must have taken them several hours to assemble all this luggage.

'We're going to fairyland, daddy.'

'Now, this minute? Can't you wait till mum gets back? I know she'd want to say goodbye to you.'

They went into a huddle and whispered together. At last Emily said: 'We have to go now.'

'How do you expect to take all these bags? Fairies only have wings; they don't have cargo planes.'

Kate said: 'There'll be enough fairies to take a bag each.'

So this was where too many charming Edwardian books about flower fairies could land the unsuspecting parent.

'Kate dear, what should I tell your mother when she comes to collect you and finds you gone?'

'That I'm in fairyland of course.'

Being five years older, Lucy realised the fix I was in and said to Emily: 'You won't be able to see mum and dad in fairyland. Grown-ups aren't allowed.'

'I'll come back and visit.'

'That's not allowed either,' I improvised. 'And you won't see Jess and Lucy any more.'

I sensed that the two of them were pushing their fantasy as far as they could, while knowing deep down that if they went out into the street a swarm of fairies was unlikely to sweep them up into the clouds with all their Sainsbury's bags. Yet, at the same time, they felt this just *might* happen if they backed their belief and went through with it. I felt as if I was facing that awful Tinkerbell question in Peter Pan, 'Do you believe in fairies?', when parents are expected to shout back 'Yes!' along with their children. Was I to be forced to yell back 'No', or could I pour just enough cold water on them to check their present enterprise, while letting them keep their fantasy in tact? Although I just managed the balancing act, for Emily the fantasy was almost at an end.

One evening a week later, with other things on my mind, I forgot to remove one of her milk teeth from under her pillow, causing her a crisis of faith. The following afternoon, having discussed with a friend the meaning of this shocking event, she asked me point blank:

'Are you the tooth fairy, daddy?'

'Rather a forgetful one, I'm afraid.'

Even if my father hadn't regularly surprised me with remarks implying the continuance of an inner life, I would have gone on visiting, even after he stopped recognizing me. His body, while living, was like a shrine to the man he had been. Sometimes I brought an offering of soft fruit, and gave him strawberries or squares of melon in a spoon. He would eat with enjoyment, without having any idea who was feeding him.

One day, I arrived at the Royal Free and was shocked to find him spearing some grey and nameless lumps of meat with his fork. It seemed a cruel mockery of his lifelong stand. I went in search of the staff nurse at once to ask her to see to it that in future he was given only vegetarian food. She seemed puzzled by my concern.

'I'm not trying to make excuses,' she told me, promptly making one. 'He's down as a veggie. But if he doesn't know what he's eating, what does it matter?'

'You'd respect a dead man's wish to be cremated, so why not a living man's wish to eat no meat?'

'I can't really say.'

'Can you guarantee the same thing won't happen again?'

She told me I could depend on her while she was on the ward which might be for a month.

Because I told people my father wouldn't recognize them, he had few visitors during the last six months of his life. Only three friends from the Order of the Cross, and I, went on visiting him until he died. The Order owned a house in woodland near Newbury, and a friend sent him a postcard depicting it. 'Dear Clifford, You will remember the cedar tree at Snelsmore House and will think of the slopes of Lebanon. "O Love of God, so great, so true, / In Thee my Being I renew." Love from Queenie.'

When walking my retriever on the Heath each day, I saw the stark outline of the hospital rising up behind the trees like the superstructure of a vast ship. At dusk the lights glowed palely in the plate-glass windows, and I imagined my father lying, eyes closed, on the seventh floor – only now, it wasn't him any more. And I thought how fast I would run to the hospital, if suddenly learning that he was really to be found somewhere inside that dying, emaciated body.

My father began to refuse food a month after the meat incident. I was telephoned by his consultant and asked whether I wanted him to be fed through a tube. I discussed this with my sister and we gave our consent to his receiving only fluids. We felt it would have been too upsetting for my mother to have been asked to make this decision. I went in each day to see that he was not in pain, and that his mouth and lips were being kept moist. Near the end, I kissed him on the forehead, and recalled him saying when I was a child that bodies were only vehicles for souls – at the time it had made me think of those Dinky toy cars that had model drivers inside. I had a strong sense that he had gone from here already, leaving behind an empty case in his old shape, the way caterpillars do before becoming butterflies. But I still didn't want the phone to ring and to hear the news that was inevitable. He was still alive – still my father. He died in the early evening of 19 November 1986.

All he had taken in with him had been a few clothes and a top denture, as I would find when I was handed a list of these things. This was when I collected his death certificate. I then drove to see my mother at Woodstock.

'He still gets letters,' she told me, indicating a pile of junk mail which she had preserved. I opened the top one. 'Dear Mr Jeal, There's never been a better time to apply for your Barclaycard . . .'

Before my father was even buried, my mother insisted on going through the contents of his desk with me. Photographs of them both when younger; a few letters from her to him – I took in the odd phrase: 'You looked a perfect pet shaving, with white fluff on your face, and *such* an intent look.' My mother held up a photograph of him wearing his army cap. 'I can't seem to take in that he's dead.'

Two items were especially evocative, one was the piece of wood with a ball on top, which during my childhood he had attempted to grip with his toes to improve the condition of his feet. The other was a photograph of him taken at school in Dorking, aged fifteen. Gazing at this attractive boy who had possessed my father's might-have-beens, I seemed to catch a glimpse of the mystery governing all our destinies.

I made a mess of telling my children about 'grandpa's' death. Even as I was on the telephone telling a cousin the 'sad news' ('a blessing really', blah, blah), seven-year-old Emily passed the half-open door. I did not see her, but heard her scream as if she had been stabbed in the heart.

About two weeks later, when I went to kiss her goodnight, she talked a lot about death and her fear that granny would die soon, and about the oddness of having 'my little life and doing so many things and then being nothing'. Then she reminded me of grandpa running on the lawn, and said how wonderful it would be if we went into a shop and suddenly saw him young again and in perfect health.

'I'd like you and mum to stay forty and stop having birthdays; then when I reach forty we'll be the same age. I'd like us all to die on the same day.' After a pause, she looked at me with interest: 'Are you crying, daddy?' I didn't answer. 'I've never seen you cry before.'

At my father's funeral I read aloud two meditations he had written many years earlier.

Reality is not a possession come at through striving. It is a state of being wherein all striving has departed. It is rest from striving . . . It is tranquillity, yet full of intensity. There is no possession in reality: it possesses us rather – we become part of it, freed from all fear and from all craving.

My life is valuable to God as His Own Life. He will direct or use it as He wishes. I will fulfil His design . . . The call sometimes appears as too much, as unnatural . . . But I shall be ready. God will prepare me in the right moment . . . We are not the slaves of God, but divinity in the making.

# SIXTEEN

Like most children, I once had immense faith in the protective powers of my parents. But while I never doubted that they would be around forever, I knew from the age of six that my father was fallible. On one of our many walks to Kensington Gardens via De Vere Gardens – where we would often drop in at the headquarters of the Order of the Cross – I saw in the window of a toyshop at the end of Launceston Place a little tin steamship with a red funnel. For a week or two my father held out against my pleas to be bought this beautiful ship.

'Some boy with a richer daddy will buy it soon,' I said pressing my forehead against the glass.

But no richer daddy ever did pass by and wreck my dream, and in the end my histrionics paid off and my father allowed himself to be bullied into buying the red-funnelled steamer. I sang to myself and danced along, clutching a thrilling oblong box, bound for the Broad Walk and the Round Pond. In the past I had quite enjoyed watching other children's boats, but never had I known such happiness as I felt today, approaching the water's edge.

My steamship had a metal rudder, which if set to one side at the correct angle would bring her back to land again just before the clockwork mechanism wound down completely. At least a dozen successful trips had been made by the time my father announced that we would be late for supper unless we left Kensington Gardens at once.

'That's all for now, Tim.'

'Just one more trip,' I begged, shoving the boat into the water anyway. In my haste, I failed to set the rudder at the proper angle and my little vessel headed straight out towards the centre of the pond.

'Get a stick!' cried my father, knowing the boat must be plucked from the water immediately. But there were only a few miserable twigs to be seen. And there was my father, still sitting on a bench taking off his shoes, while my ship was almost beyond the point where she could be grabbed by anyone paddling.

'Please get in the water now!'

Unfortunately for me, his Herbert Barker shoes were worth vastly more than the boat, and he did not intend to get them wet. It was agony for me to see him losing yet more time struggling to undo the laces of his second shoe.

'Hurry, daddy!'

But even as I spoke, I knew it was too late to wade in. I let out a wail which sent my poor father dashing to the edge, where he stood balancing awkwardly on his one shod foot, while his naked one waved about in the air – a picture of dithering indecision.

'Maybe the wind will blow it in again,' he said, hopping back to the bench to put on his discarded shoe.

Somewhere out there, roughly in the middle of that vast pond, my steamer's propeller ceased to rotate.

There were always a number of 'boy men' at the pond, owners of magnificent yachts so large that they had to be wheeled to the water on trolleys. Because most of these boyish grown-ups stepped into the water to stop their boats hitting the pond's edge, they wore thigh-length boots. Although my father did his best to persuade them to take pity on us, all refused, saying the water in the middle would come over the top of their waders. But there was a rowing boat in a shed near the Orangery, and they said that for a fee of £2 a boatman would wheel this boat to the pond and rescue my helpless steamer.

My father raised a hand to his brow. £2 was a huge sum – far more than he had paid for my steamer.

'Do you think it's been blown in any closer?' he asked, gazing hopefully into the distance.

'I think we should fetch that man.'

My father looked at his watch and, because we were already late for supper, reckoned he had little to lose by waiting till the breeze blew in my boat. That way he would not have to pay £2 or buy a replacement vessel. But, as the light began to fade, the wind dropped, and my boat became motionless on the glassy surface of the pond. By the time we went in search of the boatman, he had gone home.

So my father had achieved the worst possible outcome, for me at any rate. I returned home in tears, without my steamship, to be told that our supper was inedible, though I seem to remember eating it.

Lying in bed, I imagined how the fathers of several school friends would have behaved in the same crisis. All would either have got their shoes wet, or paid the £2. If only my father could turn himself into a bustling, young, car-owning, thick-haired, decisive father.

The following morning when I woke up and looked around, I wondered if I was still asleep. My steamship was propped at the end of my bed. I reached out and touched it. In the dining room my mother told me quite matter-of-factly that after I had gone to bed, my father had returned to the pond with a torch. By now he would have left for work, so I wouldn't be able thank him till the evening.

'What on earth's the matter with you?' asked my mother, noticing how stricken I looked. 'You've got your boat back, haven't you?'

Five months after my father died, my mother telephoned me with the news that Johnny Brown was ill and could not move his back legs.

'Please come at once. He must see a vet soon.'

I could not leave immediately because Joyce was out in the car, but I expected her back within the hour. Before that, my old adversary, the chairman of the trust rang to say she 'happened to have heard' from a member of staff that Johnny wasn't well. She didn't sound pleased, but she didn't sound sorry either.

'I trust you'll see this sad event as an opportunity.'

'You've lost me.'

'An opportunity to end the cat problem.'

'I wasn't aware that there was one.'

'Try to be sensible, Mr Jeal. Imagine what it will be like if the animal becomes incontinent.'

I promised to try to imagine it and rang off. Joyce came home ten minutes later, and I drove to Woodstock with a cat basket on the passenger seat beside me. My prayer as I entered the house was that I would somehow be able to persuade my mother not to come with me and the cat. It was horrible to think of Johnny being given a lethal injection with her holding him.

I had feared that Johnny might howl pitifully when I put him in the basket, but he was too groggy even to meow.

'You'll be fine, Johnny, darling,' my mother told him,

though he looked anything but fine, with his eyes swivelling back and forth and his tongue sticking out.

I took my mother's hand and said very solemnly: 'I promise to do everything I can to see he comes back safely.'

My mother gave me a look of profound scepticism. 'You needn't think you're going there alone with him.'

'Why not?'

'Because I mean to have a chat with the vet.'

'Couldn't you tell me what to say?'

'No, I couldn't.'

In the car, she became emotional, referring to Johnny as her 'closest friend' and even her 'only friend', and then glared at me as if daring me to contradict her.

My mother said: 'I expect you think I should have him put down anyway.'

'That's totally unfair.'

'I'm not idiotic. I know if he doesn't get better, he'll have to be put down. But I want them to do their best. That's all.'

'I want him to get better too.'

As we waited our turn – behind a boxer dog, a yapping corgi, two other cats in baskets, and all their owners – my mother shielded Johnny with her body from these people and their pets. I felt sick with the tension of what might happen next. We could enter the surgery and be told within seconds that Johnny had to be destroyed. What a drive back to Woodstock we would have without him.

As soon as we were in the surgery, my mother advanced on the vet. She looked small, pugnacious, and yet very vulnerable.

'He's my only real friend, so I'd rather you didn't kill him unless there's absolutely no alternative.'

'We'll certainly do what we can.' The vet smiled reassuringly. 'Let's have a look at him, shall we?'

So I opened the basket and took the cat out. His glazed

eyes were still flicking back and forth, incredibly quickly. The vet only needed to glance at him to see he'd had a stroke. He told us so at once.

'Johnny thinks the world is moving from right to left at about thirty miles per hour. So he's trying to keep it still. That's why his eyes are moving from side to side like that.'

'What are his chances?' whispered my mother. 'Or would it be kinder to . . .?' I stared at the floor, preparing myself for the worst.

The vet surprised us both by smiling. 'I'd say his chances are slightly better than 50-50. So what we'll do is keep him here and see that he doesn't fall about and hurt himself, or become dehydrated. Then if you ring me on Monday, we'll see how he is then.'

My mother stroked Johnny thankfully. His fur was matted and dry-looking. Seeing my mother in her threadbare, pink overcoat, which she refused to throw out, stroking her sick cat, I remembered her with Selina, her sleek Siamese, looking happy and well-dressed in the mid-1950s. A lot could happen to a person in a few decades, even during a supposedly uneventful life.

On Monday, I took some deep breaths and telephoned the vet. To my delight, I was told that Johnny had made a remarkable recovery.

'He'll be able to use a litter tray?'

'He's doing that already, and eating well.'

I couldn't resist ringing the trust's chairman to share the good news with her, before going down to Woodstock to tell my mother in person.

When my mother was in her fifties, she engaged a professional photographer to take some studio portraits. She came back rather pleased with herself.

'It was expensive,' she told me, 'but one day you'll be glad.'

I didn't see these photographs until a few years later, and was horrified. The man had retouched them so extensively that his subject was almost unrecognisable. Luckily, several pictures I chanced to take in our back garden with my extremely unsophisticated camera have preserved her friendly, open smile.

To the best of my knowledge, my mother remained faithful to my father throughout their marriage; but once or twice, I think I detected wistfulness. When I was fifteen, my adventurous, happy-go-lucky cousin, Mona (then in her Bohemian late fifties), drove me to the south of France for an exchange with a French family she knew near Carcassone. She drove me in her Renault *Dauphine* with her lover of many years, Roland Preece, who had been shot down in the Great War while serving in the Royal Flying Corps. Afterwards, in an unfortunate chapter of accidents, he had married someone else though still loving Mona. He was charming, cultivated, softly spoken, and hugely sympathetic to women of his generation.

When he and Mona were happily packing the car, watched by my mother, she appeared to be genuinely glad for them – Roland's wife was still alive, so he and Mona were rarely able to be together. Before I got into the car too, my mother thrust upon me a striped towelling dressing gown which she said I would be sure to need on the Riviera. I kissed her goodbye, and for a moment saw her gaze with unexpected soulfulness at Roland. It came back to me that she had dressed and made-up more carefully than usual when we had stayed with Roland and his wife in Ireland two years earlier, and that my father had been dismayed when Roland had given her a large blue and white Stilton cover and a silk scarf. But gifts or no gifts, my mother knew she had never lived an adventurous life like Mona, nor kicked over the traces, and had just one blissful liaison.

That night we arrived in Beauvais and could find only one unoccupied room in the town. I found myself sharing a single bed with Roland, while Mona curled up, uncomplaining, in a child's cot. We laughed a lot on that journey, and drank a lot too. At Carcassone, Mona left me with my French family, before driving on with Roland to Cannes. Seeing them waving goodbye so happily, I thought of my mother in London.

But I was soon engrossed by other things. Sputnik was whizzing round the globe at the time, and was plainly visible on clear nights from the south of France. On most evenings, I would sit on the beach, not wearing that dressing gown, with the children of my French family (all slightly older than me) and listen to American pop songs like 'Tutti Frutti' and 'Only the Lonely'. Why on earth hadn't I appreciated them before? I was taught to ride a scooter and to kiss with my mouth open. I hardly gave my mother another thought until I got home again, and was welcomed with her usual enthusiasm and love.

A year after my father's death, I visited his grave in Hampstead Cemetery. It was the first time since his funeral. A few weeks earlier, an unusually powerful storm had uprooted many trees on Hampstead Heath, and now a great Stock Market crash was front page news. I didn't take these events for omens – though perhaps I should have done. On the day of my father's funeral, his grave had been on the edge of a pleasant area of open grass. In a single year, the frontier of death had rolled across this virgin sward, leaving it littered with grubby mounds of overturned earth, rotting flowers and brand new tombstones, some as shiny black as the cars my father had never owned. A few older, grander graves stood nearby. With their weeping angels and wrought iron, they seemed to look down on their cheaper modern equivalents.

My father's headstone was white marble with the lettering chased-in in lead. This job had been done so meticulously that, at first, I thought the mason had saved money by using black paint; but on running a finger over the surface, I was reassured. His name was spelled correctly, his dates the right ones, and his optimistic words recorded just as he had written them: 'We are not the slaves of God, but divinity in the making.' Beneath was a gap, large enough for my mother's name, her dates, and for a second quotation if my sister or I could think of one when the time came.

I rested my hand on the stone and thought about my father's slow fade-out from life, which had been so upsetting to us all. Yet I now saw that in one respect the process had been merciful. As his mental disintegration had progressed, he had become less and less conscious of being incapacitated, or even ill.

My father had often said that nothing happened by chance in life, and that his illness had been God's chosen means to reclaim him. Standing there among the graves, I wished I could hear his voice again, even if only to repeat to me this repugnant notion.

'You ought to read Kant's "transcendental hypothesis",' my father had told me in my late twenties, after a rare religious chat, in which I had dismissed human immortality. Not long after his death, I found a sheet of paper on which he'd written out a passage attributed to Kant. The opening proposition was that, since human births usually arose from trivial causes like lust and opportunity, it was hard to argue that such casually started existences ought rationally to be accorded the dignity of immortality:

> 'But to meet this objection,' argued Kant, 'we can propound a transcendental hypothesis: by seeing this world as a mere dream or picture of the purely spiritual life, we perceive things as they really are, and see ourselves as spiritual beings in an eternal community which did not begin with birth and will not cease with bodily death . . .'

Although Kant had deliberately set himself the task of finding a way to make immortality seem credible, I still felt quite attracted by his idea. My past *did* sometimes seem like a dream or picture of somewhere else – a place in which all the bizarre personalities had indeed always existed and could not simply disappear. I caught myself glancing skywards, as I left the cemetery.

When I got home, Lucy and a friend were watching a romantic film on television in which the hero and heroine were kissing hungrily. The soundtrack was far too loud.

'Dad,' gasped Lucy, 'did you ever do that?'

'Oh, yuck,' groaned her friend, 'he's eating her lips!'

'Do Jess and Sean kiss like that?' demanded Lucy, seeming to think I would be more likely to tell her about Jessica's and her new boyfriend's habits than about my own.

'Well, do they?' echoed the friend.

'I expect so.'

'Ha, ha!' muttered Lucy.

Ages ago, my mother's impatience with similar films had suggested that she too found physical passion improbable. But the need for warmth and companionship had not been so easy to do without. 'The grave's a fine and private place, / And none, I think, do there embrace.' No wonder my mother missed my father more than I had imagined she would.

Once she said to me: 'I know he's gone, but I can't *feel* that he has. I still expect to find him sitting in his chair.'

After my father's death, my mother would gaze ahead of her fixedly and would very rarely smile. She never said she was depressed, nor appealed for sympathy, but later I found a scrap of paper on which she had scrawled her misery. Whatever their differences, in some mysterious way my father had been vital to her well-being, and none of the rest of us could help her.

One grey November afternoon I drove her around Regent's Park, where many storm-felled trees were still lying about, and brought her home for supper. In the past few months she had been struggling to keep up her interest in all of us, but now I sensed a lassitude verging on indifference. A year ago she had still been writing to Coutt's with instructions to send her money in a registered envelope, just as she always had done, starting her letters 'Gentlemen'. (Possibly her manager had been a woman by then.) But now she depended upon me to bring her money. She liked to have some to hand, so she could tip her visiting hairdresser – this being her last obeisance to the customs of a past she no longer wanted to recall or even talk about. Her greatest pleasures had been entertaining, giving presents, tending her garden, enjoying her collection of pictures, and visiting her friends who ran a nearby antique shop. All this independence now lay behind her, and reminiscence only seemed to rub this in. On one occasion, trying to cheer her up, I mentioned the toughness of her naval ancestors.

'Bugger my ancestors,' she exploded.

Christmas had upset her for several years because she couldn't get to the shops to buy presents for her grandchildren and she hated relying on other people to choose them for her. A year ago she had been eager to send Christmas cards, but this year she had found it a great bore, though, with my sister's encouragement, she had written out several dozen cards in the end.

I visited my mother in the first week of December, when the television news was filled with pictures of the King's Cross fire. I sat with her and we watched smoke billowing up from the underground's escalators onto the main-line concourse.

My mother said: 'Anyone going by tube, who can afford a taxi, must be out of their minds.'

'You quite often went by tube,' I reminded her.

'And hated every moment of it.'

I glanced at the screen. 'At least nothing like *that* ever happened to you.'

'I hope you're not asking me to count my blessings?' She eyed me fiercely. 'If there are no taxis in the afterlife, I'll be giving it a miss.'

Then she turned off the television and we talked about other things, all of them inconsequential, which I greatly regret since this was to be the last time I saw her.

On 11 December, she telephoned me at about half-past two in the morning.

'I feel awful, Tim. I don't seem able to catch my breath.'

Still half asleep, I supposed she had bronchitis or a chest infection, and completely failed to grasp the significance of her words. Instead of offering to come to see her at once, as I should have done, I said: 'I'll ring Dr Peters first thing in the morning and come myself at about nine.'

After ringing off, I took the phone into the sitting room so I could telephone the care assistant on duty, without keeping Joyce awake. I asked the woman to go and see my mother and ring me back, which she did five minutes later, saying that my mother seemed to have indigestion and that she would give her something for it. She promised to telephone me if she was in any distress later in the night. I then spoke to my mother again to be told that she felt 'a little better but still not right'.

'What'll happen to Johnny if Dr Peters thinks I should go into hospital?'

'I'll have Johnny to stay with me here, or Mary will take him for a while. You probably won't need to go in anyway.'

And then we both said goodnight.

Assuming that Joyce would be asleep again by now, I didn't return to our bedroom but went upstairs to the spare room. Exhausted and not thinking straight, I forgot to take the phone with me to the top of our tall, thin house.

At quarter to six I was woken by someone ringing the doorbell and then knocking loudly. Joyce was already on her way down, and I caught up with her in the hall. We looked at one another for a moment before I opened the door.

Two policemen stood on the steps. 'Are you Mr Timothy Jeal?' one of them asked me, as if I had committed a crime.

'Yes, I am.'

'Can we come in, sir?' I retreated a few steps, allowing them to enter. The four of us stood in the hall very close to one another. 'I'm sorry, sir, but I have some bad news for you. Your mother, Norah Jeal, died at four o'clock this morning. The people at the Home tried to reach you by phone but couldn't raise you.'

When they had gone, Joyce and I wept together in the kitchen. I was haunted by the thought that my mother might have telephoned again in the night and the phone have rung unheard in the sitting room. At seven, I called my sister, only remembering that it was her birthday as I was breaking the news to her.

I thought I would find my mother's body still in her bed when I went down to Woodstock shortly before eight. But I was too late. I dimly remembered hearing that the staff always tried to have the dead removed when few people were about. That way elderly residents were not reminded of their own mortality.

At the head of the empty bed, sitting up very straight on my mother's pillow, was her faithful Johnny, who, unlike me, had been with her at the end.

# SEVENTEEN

Because my mother had been alive on every night of my life until the moment I last spoke to her, I had assumed she would manage to stay alive for a few nights more. This was not a mistake I would ever be able to put right. It consoled me a little to think that if I had gone to Woodstock that night and had found my mother dying, I would very likely have lacked the wisdom and courage to let her die. By calling an ambulance, I would probably only have ensured that her last hours were passed in the organized frenzy of an accident and emergency department.

Later in the morning I returned for Johnny with a basket. I was tempted to take him home with me, but since I owned a dog and two cats, one of them eighteen years old and tetchy, it seemed fairer to ask Mary to take him for a fee. She had been feeding Johnny for six months and cared about him. (He would only survive my mother by a month.)

In the post that brought the first letters of condolence, I recognized my mother's hand. Inside the envelope was her Christmas card – a robin at the centre of a wreath of holly. No special words. 'Love from Norah. Hope you all have a very happy Christmas.'

When I'd first been sent away to school, I'd begged her to write to me in block capitals because I couldn't read her writing. She had agreed reluctantly. Her governess had never taught her to spell, she explained, so she only managed to conceal her misspellings by writing illegibly. In time I'd learned to read her writing like a form of shorthand. This card was the last example I would ever receive.

Until the last two or three months of her life, my mother's mood had always brightened when I reminded her of some comical or bizarre story from the past. One that had always made her laugh immoderately concerned one of the rare occasions on which my father had felt impelled to take a taxi somewhere. On the afternoon in question, he had returned home from work to find himself so hopelessly late for a 'meet the teachers' session at Westminster that no alternative form of transport was open to him. My mother had set out for the school half-an-hour earlier and had left an angry note urging him to hurry, so he ran out into the Cromwell Road and in pouring rain managed to catch a cab – a remarkable achievement during a wet rush-hour.

At the very moment of his success, a middle-aged black man splashed towards him through the puddles and rapped on the glass, before passionately pleading to be allowed to take the taxi since he was late for a concert.

'Maybe we could share it?' suggested my father, very loath to surrender the cab, but already wavering as he sensed a need greater than his own. 'Where are you going?'

'The Royal Festival Hall,' replied the man.

'Hop in,' said my father, thankfully. 'We're going in the same direction.'

They had barely reached Gloucester Road when my father's fellow passenger opened the small leather case he had been clutching, and lifted from its velvet nest a glistening silver harmonica.

'I'm Sonny Boy Williamson,' he declared, 'and because you saved my life back there, I'm gonna give you your own concert.'

So, all the way to Westminster, while the rain beat down on the roof of the cab, my father was treated to his own command performance by the world's most famous blues harmonica player.

Given their many misunderstandings over the years, the fact that my father's death made such a profound impact on my mother is greatly to her credit and to his. Being of a completely different cast of mind, my mother never took much pleasure in his 'Great Thoughts Calendar', when he tore off and read out the day's quotation at breakfast. But one morning I remember him declaiming: 'Blessedness is not the reward of virtue, it is virtue itself,' and my mother surprised me by saying, 'That's really rather good.'

Only once can I remember her being amused by a religious comment made by my father, but this one instance made her laugh many times, although the joke was on her too. In those dismal days when the number of her cats was ballooning into the mid-teens, my mother sometimes lost count of exactly how many animals she had. One afternoon, I was at home in north London, when the telephone rang.

'I'm really sorry to trouble you, but can you come over fairly soon? You know my little back and white cat, Smudge?'

'I don't remember him.'

'He's a her, actually. Well, she's been run over.'

'Where is she?'

'On the road over the bridge. Her body's in the gutter. You know I hate asking favours, but will you please come now and bury poor Smudge in the garden. Joe can't manage, and I simply can't face it.'

Since my mother had sounded so wretched, I came and collected the cat, which was still in the gutter, and to my relief had not been squashed. *Rigor mortis* had set in and the cat's legs were stuck out straight, as if she was made of wood under her fur. I took her back to the house, dug a grave in the garden near the bay tree, and covered her. My mother watched tearfully as I patted down the earth. She seemed so distressed that I offered to stay on for a while, but she wouldn't let me. So with parental plaudits ringing in my ears, I drove home again, knowing the blessedness of virtue – or some transitory approximation.

Later that same afternoon, my father telephoned me. He had just looked out of the sitting room window and seen Smudge sitting in the flowerbed on top of her own grave.

'It's like the Resurrection,' he told me, joyfully, before ringing off.

Minutes later, my phone went again. My mother could hardly speak for laughter. Smudge had just walked into the kitchen and demanded her supper.

'All the time, she was somewhere down the road,' gasped my mother. 'I'm afraid you've just buried . . .' more helpless laughter, 'a complete stranger.'